THE DRUIDS

Stuart Piggott

with 130 illustrations, 16 in color

Thames and Hudson

Ancient Peoples and Places
GENERAL EDITOR: GLYN DANIEL

© 1968 and 1975 Stuart Piggott

Published in the USA in 1985 by Thames and Hudson Inc.,
500 Fifth Avenue, New York, New York 10110

Library of Congress Catalog Card Number 84-51870

Printed and bound in the German Democratic Republic

THE DRUIDS

CONTENTS

A full-length book on the Druids, involving as it would detailed studies in many disciplines, including those of prehistory, classical literature and the history of ideas, could hardly be written by one scholar. It was thought however that a short synoptic treatment of the varied source-material was worth while attempting and not impossible to achieve. I have offered such a survey here, and while keenly aware of its inadequacies hope that it may serve to explain the Druids to the general reader, and to present them in credible and understandable form.

My indebtedness to others is great, and in part indicated in the bibliography. Two Celtic scholars have given me help and encouragement at every turn, Professor K.H. Jackson and Dr Anne Ross, and both have placed me further in their debt by reading the book in draft form and making invaluable critical comments. Professor A. M. Snodgrass has similarly read chapter III. In general the book owes much to conversations over the years with Professor R. J. C. Atkinson, Mr H. M. Colvin, Professor G. E. Daniel and the late Professor T. G. E. Powell.

S. P.

Chapter One

THE PROBLEMS AND THE SOURCES

The visitor to the ancient monument of Stonehenge, on Salisbury Plain in southern England, may well encounter a remarkable spectacle at the time of the Summer Solstice. If he is there around sunrise on June 21st or at noon on that day, he may find a grave body of white-robed men and women engaged in ceremonies and processions among the stones, and if he enquires, will be told that they are The Druids.

If he gives the matter further thought he may well ask himself the question 'Who are these Ancient People, and are they in their rightful Ancient Place?' The answer is not a simple one. It involves archaeology and ancient history; literary sources in classical and Celtic languages; the history of ideas and of literary and artistic fashions from the last few centuries up to yesterday. It is also bedevilled with almost unbelievably fatuous speculations and fantasies, and shot through and through with (in Leacock's famous phrase) Moonbeams from the Larger Lunacy. This book tries to present a sober account of a subject all too often given a cosy place among the Comforts of Unreason.

Perhaps it may be asked why an uncertainty should present itself at this point. The Druids have in fact achieved a place in the average Englishman's mind as part of his heritage, set with Magna Carta or Cavaliers and Roundheads in a misty perspective where Hampton Court, Stonehenge or Chatsworth can act as a back-cloth as required. The more knowledgeable may remember that Julius Caesar wrote about them; the less critical may accept the unbroken survival of the priesthood until today. Like the past, they are felt to be only marginally interesting, and are accepted without more thought than is allotted to the rest of what passes for history in most persons' minds.

But the Druids do, in fact, have a remarkable interest as a phenomenon, for in the form they are seen today they are the end-product of a long story which illuminates in the most fascinating way, how a consistent and recurrent pattern of thought, emotion and belief about some of mankind's eternal problems can persist to worry thinkers from Hesiod in Greece of the eighth century B C to modern writers of science fiction on both sides of the Atlantic. Quite apart from the archaeology of Early Iron Age Europe and the nature of pagan Celtic religion, we shall have in this book to consider the Golden Age and News from Nowhere; the Noble Savage and the Fall from Grace; natural wisdom and remotely-dwelling superior intelligences.

The Druid story has in part an evidential basis of observation and comment; this can in turn be brought into critical relationship with what we know or deduce of ancient Celtic religion from texts and iconography, and to what we tentatively infer of ceremony and ritual from the evidence of archaeology. Using this group of evidence we can form a picture of the Druids as a part of the prehistoric Celtic priesthood which is internally consistent and intrinsically credible, if neither very edifying in content nor elevating in character. On the other hand, the understanding of, and comments on, the barbarians around them by the classical *literati* were inevitably coloured by contemporary modes of thought and current philosophical schemes, and here we enter the world of the history of ideas, and must endeavour to detect where concepts and motifs have been unconsciously imposed on the Druids by those who first wrote about them, and who on occasion did them the honour of finding in them convenient vehicles for the exemplification of a philosophical concept.

When we come to the discovery of the prehistoric past from the Renaissance onwards, and the incidental rediscovery of the Druids, we find them re-created by men who were themselves steeped in the philosophy and scholarship of the Greek and Roman thinkers who had first commented upon this obscure barbarian priesthood. The climate of thought was congenial to an acceptance and a development of the classical philosophers' view, and when fashion shifted from classical to romantic, the Druids were quietly waiting to take on a new life in the contemporary modes of Western thought and emotion. And so, as curiously satisfactory symbols, they have kept their place for a couple of thousand years or more: barbarian sages, primeval Christians, champions of liberty, repositories of mysterious wisdom. One of our main tasks will be to disentangle the component strands in the twisted Druidic skein, and to ask ourselves questions about certain assumptions.

It would seem reasonable to ask one question at the outset – why has a priesthood within the barbarian pre-Roman Celtic religion, attested by a handful of some thirty scrappy references in Greek and Roman authors, many little-known and some downright obscure, come even to be remembered at all except by scholars nearly two thousand years after its official suppression by Roman authority? This in itself is surely so odd as to merit investigation in its own right. But there are other reasons which make the enquiry attractive as an intellectual adventure, and these are implicit in the very nature of the problems presented to us by the Druids.

I have already indicated that our problems fall into two main groups – those concerned with what we may fairly call the factual basis for our knowledge of the Druids, and those involved with the unconscious or conscious creation of Druid idealizations or myths. Using the philosophical approach to our knowledge of the human past of R. G. Collingwood, we can distinguish (as we shall see later) a past-in-itself to which all historians (or prehistorians) address themselves, but by reason of its being in fact the past, they can never attain. What they perceive and construct is a past-as-known within the limitations of the evidence available, and their own capabilities, inadequacies and background. What, however, can also be constructed is that very dangerous thing, a past-as-wished-for, in which a convenient selection of the evidence is fitted into a predetermined intellectual or emotional pattern. And so with the ancient Druids – we have the Druids-in-themselves, whom we can never reach, but for whom we have literary and archaeological evidence from which we infer our Druids-as-known. There has also been a process of manufacturing Druids-as-wished-for going on since classical times. Our two groups of problems have therefore inherently different qualities – they are very roughly the outcome of objective and subjective thinking respectively.

We have, therefore, to work with three types of source material. In the first place there is archaeological evidence from graves, or from sites best interpreted as ceremonial, or from representations in Celtic or Romano-Celtic art depicting cult scenes or personages. Inferences as to likely ceremonial and ritual practices can tentatively be made from tombs or sanctuary sites; iconography can be linked to the written tradition by the intermediary discipline of epigraphy and the study of inscriptions associated with cult representations. In the second place we have the *testimonia* of the Greek and Roman writers on the Celts, their customs and religion, and that part of their priestly élite sometimes denominated Druids. As a gloss on these texts, we have the surviving fragments of an originally oral tradition in the Celtic vernaculars, transmitted by medieval Christian scribes and scholars. Finally, we have the development of ideas about the Druids originating in the antiquarian speculations of the seventeenth and eighteenth centuries, rapidly becoming part of the background material not only of scholars, but of imaginative writers and artists, and latterly developing into a folk-lore of its own among the credulous.

This tripartite nature of the evidence (as characteristically ambiguous and tortuous as any Celtic statement in triad form!) obviously calls for the most careful handling of the sources. But its interdisciplinary quality gives it an added fascination and presents a challenge, even if it has perhaps deterred some of the more cautious scholars of recent times. But it did not deter Sir Thomas Kendrick who, fifty years ago, wrote the only general account of the problem which has deserved serious attention since that date, and more than that, has stood up quite remarkably well to over a generation's active work in the fast-moving subject of pre-history. Mrs Chadwick's recent study (1966) deals only with the evidence in the classical writers. I think, however, there is room for a new treatment of that whole complex of problems which then engaged Kendrick's brilliant mind, and if my book shows its indebtedness to his on every page. I hope I may perhaps in the end be thought to have added here and there a useful, or even sometimes a percipient footnote to *The Druids* of 1927.

THE SOURCES: THE ARCHAEOLOGICAL EVIDENCE

If we consider the main fields in which potential new evidence for a knowledge of the Druids could have come to light since the late 1920's, that of archaeology is an obvious claimant. New excavations and new interpretations have enormously enlarged our knowledge of European prehistory over the past forty years, and while the gaps in our know-ledge are still lamentably large and constantly recurrent, and the depths of our sheer ignorance in many directions abysmal, even the most pessimistic prehistorians would admit that something of a coherent and consistent framework does now seem to be perceptible. But before we can consider the archaeological evidence bearing on our problem, we must take a critical look at such evidence, first in general, and then within the context of our particular investigation.

There has been some discussion of the nature of archaeological evidence during the past years, partly originating within the subject itself and partly as a reflection of the parallel enquiries into our know-ledge of the past among historians. To many, however, abstract thought about the nature of the discipline in which they are engaged seems to be found not only difficult, but embarrassing, or even unnecessary, so that in the ranks of professional archaeologists the subject has not received the attention it deserves: among the general public it is hardly thought of as a problem at all. It is in fact fundamental, and as we shall see, particularly so in connection with the Druids.

We have in fact already touched on one basic aspect of this problem when we considered Druids-as-known as distinct from Druids-as-wished-for; on the one hand a picture resulting from the logical hand-ling of legitimate evidence, and on the other one constructed to fit a predetermined idea, and seen that these Druids are particular instances of a general problem, the limitations of human knowledge of the past. These limitations are inherent in the process of human apprehension, and cannot be removed – least of all by pretending they do not exist. Historians have been concerned of late about the nature of 'fact' in history, and more than one scholar has felt it is a fallacy to think of 'historical facts' existing objectively and independently of the historian and his interpretation, and even more misleading to think of a con-venient historical label, such as 'the French Revolution', not only as a 'thing' endowed with real existence, but still worse, as a self-acting agent that 'stood up and did something'. Archaeologists should enquire at least as carefully, and perhaps with even more cause, into their allied problems, and should remember a scientist's description of 'facts' as 'particular observational data relating to the past or present'.

'The raw material of prehistory is not men, but things,' as Atkinson has put it. Archaeological evidence in itself consists of the accidentally durable, and so surviving, remnants of human culture, and when observed and recognized for what it is by an archaeologist, is archaeological fact. From such facts, direct inferences may be made, which will be legitimate if, as Margaret Smith put it 'all the evidence can be empirically verified, and nothing has been added to it': the inference is 'virtually only a paraphrase of empirical observations'. This is when archaeological evidence alone is being used, when we have what Hawkes has called a text-free as opposed to a text-aided situation: in the investigation of the Druids of course the circumstances are text-aided, but in handling the archaeological evidence alone we must not use it in a logically improper manner. As we shall see, to make any correlations at all between Druids, and the archaeological material that might be attributed to them, involves assumptions and not inferences.

Using text-free archaeological evidence in an attempt to see it in meaningful terms of human activities, we must recognize straight away that the valid information it can give is strictly limited. Hawkes constructed a four-fold scale of ascending difficulty and descending validity in archaeological interpretation, beginning with technology, on which the soundest inferences can be based, and going on to subsistence-economics, more complex but still with a large measure of reliability. But the next stage, inferences on social structure, becomes far more tricky: he instanced the problem of interpreting a large isolated building in a prehistoric settlement-plan as a chief's hut, when it could as well be considered a temple, a communal meeting-hut, a barn, or none of these things. We shall in fact meet this precise problem later in the book. And when one comes to religion, and the spiritual life of a people, just what can one legitimately infer except a few platitudes so vague as to be meaningless? 'The archaeologist may find the tub, but altogether miss Diogenes,' said Wheeler characteristically, and Margaret Smith, commenting on this remark and on the 'chief's hut' problem, goes on, 'To expect an archaeologist to infer from a hut to chieftainship, or from the tub to Diogenes, is nothing less than a demand for logical alchemy. . . . It has to be acknowledged that there is no logical relation between human activity in some of its aspects and the evidence left for the archaeologist.' And least of all, we must add, when as in our present enquiry about the Druids, we are dealing with that aspect concerned with religion, belief, ritual and a priesthood. Looking for Druids is very like looking for Diogenes.

Have we in fact to adopt a completely defeatist attitude with regard to archaeological evidence for the religious activities of non-literate communities? The proliferation of articles and books on prehistoric religion in one form or another shows that many people emphatically do not take this view, but it is precisely this which makes others of us enquire more sceptically into the bases of our knowledge. The views in such works, when examined, are found almost without exception to be based not on inferences, but on assumptions not acknowledged as such. In the Palaeolithic periods, for instance, 'The modern prehistorian has started with the assumption that he knows what palaeolithic people are likely to be concerned with: fertility, hunting, magic, totemism, etc. From this starting-point he has interpreted the art on the basis of palaeolithic representations with the supposed parallels of ethnographic practices . . . in every case unsystematic and . . . drawn from widely differing peoples,' and Ucko in another field has gone on to point out that 'several basic assumptions, that have little to support them in terms of direct archaeological evidence, have been made in terms of the Mother Goddess.' Because of such assumptions, so often presented by implication as inferences from archaeological evidence, we should be cautious.

'Archaeology is incapable of dealing with myth,' wrote Fox, concerned with this very problem, 'but ritual it can . . . recover and analyse and appreciate,' taking 'ritual' in the *O.E.D.* definition of 'a prescribed order of performing a religious or other solemn service'. 'It will be clear,' he goes on, 'that only some actions in such a service leave traces; others cannot.' In other words, among these activities of mankind which can be perceived by archaeological means are those which today we would excerpt and classify as irrational and non-utilitarian (in terms of our own presuppositions of what constitutes rational and useful behaviour): these are the acts associated with religion. Much archaeological evidence for ritual, in Fox's sense, is that associated with burials, but a boundary between burial-place and sanctuary has never been set by any religion. All architecture, in the widest sense of all buildings however impermanent or primitive, is a durable three-dimensional setting for some form of human activity, static or in motion, and among human activities, as we have seen, we must include those which require sites designed as the structural setting for certain ritual performances which themselves controlled the formal planning and spatial relationships of the component elements in the composition. In a word, sanctuaries, shrines, temples and sacred enclosures should be perceptible in archaeological evidence, sometimes identifiable as such by reasonably direct inference, sometimes to be interpreted by a frank recourse to assumptions and analogues, but one hopes with an honest admission rather than an attempt to take refuge in 'logical alchemy'.

If we identify such structures with archaeological associations, a chronological position and a geographical distribution consonant with a place in Celtic material culture we may, if only to avoid the unnecessary multiplication of hypotheses, reasonably assume that they too represent an integral element of Celtic life; if there is the epigraphic evidence of inscriptions to render our archaeology momentarily text-aided, we may link a shrine to a named divinity. As no pre-Christian inscription containing the word 'Druid' has so far been discovered, any connection between this body and an archaeological site can only be an unverifiable assumption in the present state of our knowledge.

We have then some text-free archaeological evidence for Celtic religious sites, and our inference that the evidence *is* Celtic is strengthened by the documentary evidence that fortunately renders this culture and period in part text-aided archaeology. We can in fact say something about how and when certain ceremonial sites were used, but we must always remember that to all archaeological 'questions beginning "Why . . . ?", there is one short, simple and perfectly correct answer: "We do not know, and we shall probably never know."' But Atkinson, having said this, reminds us, surely rightly, that as archaeologists trying to inform the layman we have no right 'to take refuge in a smug nescience, by an appeal to the strict canons of archaeological evidence, when faced with perfectly legitimate questions of this kind', provided always that we make it abundantly clear when we do attempt such an answer that we are 'indulging in speculation upon subjects about which there is no possibility of greater certainty'.

ICONOGRAPHIC AND EPIGRAPHIC EVIDENCE

So far as the archaeological evidence for a religious order in antiquity goes, then, we must first recognize that in the nature of things it cannot be perceived by archaeology unless this is aided by some sort of literary record, notably inscriptions. But as we have seen, no authentic pre-Christian inscription includes any word for 'Druid' in the possible Greek, Latin or Celtic forms, so that their association with any field monument, sculpture or dedicatory text must remain at best an assumption. What archaeological, text-free, evidence can provide is a framework of Celtic material culture for the period and the areas within which Druidism was recorded by the classical writers. Between such evidence and these literary sources, linking one to the other, stand the dedicatory inscriptions to Celtic divinities (whether or not in a Roman guise) and the representations of these gods with or without the epigraphic identification. We must consider for a moment the nature of this iconographic evidence, which forms such a valuable adjunct to archaeology.

It can be divided into two classes, those representations directly or indirectly accompanied by inscriptions, and those without: text-aided and text-free once again. If a divinity named by a dedicatory inscription on one or more occasions has distinctive attributes, such as (if human) being horned, or triple-headed, or holding a wheel, or (if animal) is a recurrent single beast, like a boar, or a group, like the bull with three cranes, then uninscribed representations with the same attributes may have had the same names. This should not however be carried too far: it would be rash to call all horned gods Cernunnos, or even perhaps all stag-antlered ones, and a count made some years ago showed that of 374 Celtic god-names then known from inscriptions, 305 occurred only once each, and only four or five of the remainder had totals of from 20 to 30 occurrences. To confuse matters more, when barbarian and classical deities are equated in dedicatory inscriptions, one Roman god may have the basic attributes of several Celtic divinities, an extreme example being the 69 Celtic god-names joined with that of Mars. One of the most profitable approaches to these problems has been isolating iconographic types and considering their geographical distributions, and so establishing the existence of local cults and cult-centres.

Our iconographic evidence for Celtic religion almost all belongs to the latest phase, when Gaul and Britain had been incorporated in the Roman Empire, and all the inscribed material is of this period. Sculptures and other depictions of human and animal forms, representational in terms of the Celtic artistic schema, are in fact sporadically known from the sixth century B C, but it was only under direct Roman influence that sculpture (usually in stone) really became common. To a large extent this seems to have been a phenomenon parallel to the Celtic use of writing, a specifically Roman craft and so almost invariably in the Latin language: representational dedicatory or funerary sculpture was again a classical convention, and so in the Celtic world expressed itself in the basically Roman schema, the native artistic idiom coming through from time to time. In the same manner the native language shows itself behind the Roman convention in the names of the local Celtic gods, or the Vulgar Latin in the inscriptions.

As even the combined evidence from all available sources leaves our knowledge of pagan Celtic religion in a state of the most rudimentary vagueness, we are unable today to appreciate the original significance of the sculpture in stone or metal or wood that makes up our iconographic corpus. It is a waste of time thinking that we can enter the minds and share the psychological and emotional states of the early Celts. We must avoid this fallacy, and also that of projecting into Romano-Celtic sculpture, for instance, our own emotional and aesthetic presuppositions. To write of 'gaunt savage symbolism' or 'barbaric tensity and beauty'; to attribute to the Celtic sculptor 'the power to convey both a fiery inner vitality . . . and . . . a serene aloof unearthly beauty'; to describe one sculpture as that of 'a grown man, who has known and practiced a fastidious austerity'; or to say of another that 'the heavy and geometrically treated eyes and mouth give the countenance divinity that the barbarian could understand, an eerie unworldliness far removed from human experience'; to say these things is not to advance knowledge or understanding. All that the writers have done is to make personal statements about their own aesthetic sensibility, and about the accepted artistic standards of the society in which their own tastes were formed. The fact that to some of us the objects in question may be moving or terrifying, or look noble or ecstatic, should not lead us to make the unwarranted and unverifiable assumption that to an Early Iron Age barbarian of two thousand years ago they conveyed the same emotional impact. After all, no one would suppose that for instance a contemplation of recent ceremonial masks from Africa or Alaska, the New Hebrides or New Guinea, without any outside knowledge of the rituals and beliefs they served, would allow us to infer the psychological terms in which they were made and used.

It is not possible to infer religious beliefs direct from iconography alone. Representations and inscriptions imply some association between Celtic deities and animals, Cernunnos the stag-antlered man, Epona and her horse, the boar Baco and so on. But before we start thinking in simplistic terms of 'animal gods' perhaps we should pause to think of the Early Christian world, and of what, unaided by any texts, we might make of the Great Beasts of the Evangelists as they stand on the gospel-pages of Durrow or Echternach, or whether we should be much helped by the bare epigraphic statements *Imago leonis* or *Imago aquilae* that in fact accompany some of them. The Gundestrup cauldron, covered with elaborate representational scenes, is to us a problem of the same order as would be some sumptuous piece of Church silver, adorned with narrative and symbol, had we no direct knowledge of the history, mythology and hagiography it depicted, and none of the real nature of the Christian faith itself.

On the other hand, some indirect use can be made of iconographic data. Dedicatory inscriptions, with or without accompanying representations, can be used to plot the geographical boundaries of local cults, but their distribution is uneven, depending in the first place on a tradition of writing having been introduced into the area, and in the second on the local availability of stone rather than perishable materials. There are, too, other factors of social geography, like those resulting in the concentration of native dedications in Roman Britain around Hadrian's Wall. We must remember too that practically all are in Latin or Greek, and so each of these is to that extent a translation of an original unwritten Celtic religious statement. We are dealing with a situation of what has been called conditional literacy, when writing was an art restricted to a few, used only for certain purposes, and expressed, with extremely few exceptions, only in the Latin language. Of Roman Britain, Jackson has said that the Celtic (British) language 'was not a written language . . . the *only* language of writing was Latin; it would not occur to anyone to write in British, nor would they know how to do so. . . . In Roman Britain those who had enough education to know the alphabet had enough to know some Latin, and those who had none did not write at all.' The same applied to Roman Gaul, where as Whatmough wrote 'there was no common practice of writing before the Latin language was introduced, and with it the free use of the art. Hence, when people began to write at all, they did so, with hardly an exception, in Latin and in the Latin alphabet.' In Southern Gaul, however, there are a number of inscriptions in Greek letters. It is not surprising, therefore, to find inconsistencies of spelling or other divergences in names which never had a written form in their original language: the Celtic world, like the rest of barbarian Europe, was one of non-literate oral tradition, which was the time-honoured and socially approved mode for the conservation and transmission of law, genealogy, story, song and myth in the vernacular. As we shall see, the Druids were specifically concerned with the preservation and continuance of this ancient convention, which avoided the use of writing.

The most important and the most difficult group of sources is that comprising written documents, and these may be divided into two classes. In the first we may place the *testimonia* of the Greek and Roman writers relating to the Celts, their religion, and occasionally to the Druids: these last refer to restricted areas of the European continent and to Britain and not to the whole Celtic world, are scanty and scrappy, frequently in second-hand quotation, and span a period from the beginning of the second century B C to the fourth century A D. In the second division come the earlier Irish hero-tales and wonder-stories in which Druids play a part, originally embodied in an oral tradition somewhat before the fifth century A D, and preserved in early medieval recensions. References to Druids in later Celtic literature, Irish or Welsh, cannot safely be used to illuminate a subject which is essentially pre-Christian and a part of prehistoric Europe.

In both groups of sources – those in Greek or Latin, and those in Old Irish – we face the problem posed to us by all literary texts surviving from the past, in that they were composed by, and addressed to, people who because of their separation from us in time and culture, can at best be understood only by a conscious and sometimes difficult effort of mental adjustment, and may lie beyond the range of any such possibility. It would be fallacious to suppose that people are other than children of their age, conditioned by their environment and limited by the influence of their contemporary culture: the world-picture of an individual is framed within these bounds as well as influenced by age and ancestry, social position and intellectual temper, or allegiance to an ideology. Even within the comparative homogeneity of modern Western culture, we would hardly expect the same world-picture to be shared by an aged Catholic priest of noble family, a young Communist from a working-class home, an American tycoon and an ex-tribal chief of an emergent African nation. In considering our documents we must first look for the context and culture of the writers and of their audience, and the ideological and social framework within which they fitted: then we may turn to the actual words. Fortunately, for our first group of sources, the classical texts, this seems possible and very illuminating. But whereas contact of a sort with the literate and highly articulate societies of Greece and Rome can be made, what hope have we of glimpsing the mentality of those barbarian Celts whose Druids attended sacrifices and read the omens, whose bards chanted the chieftain's praises, and who listened when the hero-tales were being recited in early Ireland? To say that perhaps a reasonably parallel problem might be to have a sympathetic appreciation of the thoughts of a Pathan headman at a tribal feast on the North-Western Indian frontier may illuminate the situation by analogy, but underlines its difficulty and hardly renders it more capable of solution.

In the instance of the classical sources we must also remember that the scholars and educated men of antiquity did not, and could not, view the religious rites and observances of the barbarians, the subject of our present enquiry, with the informed detachment of a modern product of secular Western tradition. Without wishing in any way to minimize the high degree of intellectual culture they represent, the capacity of their minds, trained in abstract thought and practical affairs, or the exquisite sensibility and power of their poetry and prose, it is only fair to the writers of Greece and Rome to remember that if we are really to try to understand them apparent similarities or even what may look like identity with our own modern habits of thought may be dangerously misleading. The Mediterranean world from the fifth century B C to the early centuries A D was emphatically not our own world, and they were its products.

Their upbringing and their habits of thought and feeling did not place them in a position from which they could observe sacrifice and divination, portents, prophecies and magical ritual, as anything odd or alien. All these things were inextricably part of their own lives, and they did not see things divided into sacred and profane. They knew how important it was to 'determine the flight of crook-taloned birds, marking which were of the right by nature, and which of the left'; they offered pious sacrifices. They were deeply superstitious, and something of their own barbarian past was still rather embarrassingly with them. In Rome no longer ago than the third century B C, men and women had been ritually murdered by being buried alive in the Forum Boarium. At more than one season of the year very odd performances could be seen in the public streets, as the Salii leapt and capered, beating ancient shields and chanting magic songs in an archaic tongue, or naked youths ran with whips of skin cut from dogs and goats just sacrificed in the Lupercal cave, lashing at girls as they passed, to increase their fertility. Not far from Rome, in the grove above Lake Nemi, the King of the Wood, priest and murderer, had waited apprehensively for his successor to surprise and kill him in turn. And even that efficient military machine, the Roman Army, did not march without the sacred chicken-coops, so that auguries could be drawn from the crumbs that dribbled from the beaks of hungry hens. Within the classical world the religious performances of the Celts and other barbarians were perhaps some of their more easily understood characteristics.

On the whole, where they could be perceived, differences would presumably have been felt to be in quality rather than in kind. The importance of ritual observances in Celtic life was often commented on, but hardly deplored; Celtic deities were soon found to have good enough equivalents in the classical pantheon, and in particular, auguries and divination by Celtic priests might well be met with credence or even respectful attention. As with the early Christians confronting their barbarian pagan adversaries in later centuries, when the claim to supernatural powers of the heathen cults was freely conceded, if attributed to the operations of the Powers of Darkness, so in the pagan classical world there was not only an acceptance of the validity of alien faiths, but antagonism was confined to those occasional practices which were repugnant to its own civilized ethical code. If we ask of Celtic religion, in a famous phrase used by Gibbon in another context, 'what new provocation could exasperate the mild indifference of antiquity', the answer is human sacrifice, a practice beyond all others abhorrent by the end of the pagan era. Anything too that could be construed as 'magic' was also likely to be condemned, perhaps because of an uneasy belief in its sinister powers; magic, already lower-class and deplored by the Greeks, and ultimately the subject of successive acts of repressive legislation in Rome from the beginning of the second century AD. Unfamiliar, too, though perhaps hardly to be thought reprehensible in a society neither Greek nor Roman, would be the concept of a specifically priestly class, and the absence of that deep-rooted Mediterranean, and ultimately Oriental, symbol, the roofed monumental temple with its representational images. But against these barbarities there also appeared to the classical writers to be set concepts that they could rightly include within the term 'philosophy' as employed in antiquity, and so not only familiar, and with affinities in known Greek systems of speculation, but fascinating in their theoretical implications.

Here we shall have to investigate some aspects of the general history of ideas, especially those which have involved the idealization of primitive peoples by those of more complex societies. These include a recurrent series of speculations which seem to arise in civilized communities as the result of a subconscious guilty recognition of the inadequacy of the contemporary social order, and involve the concept of simpler and more satisfactory systems, remote either in time (Golden Ages in the past), or in place (Noble Savages at or beyond the edges of contemporary geographical knowledge). This complex of ideas has profoundly affected Western thinking and feeling since Homer and Hesiod, and by a very slight enlargement, also came to comprehend the idea of Utopian societies. It has all the vitality of a great commonplace, and today provides a theme for much science fiction for, as modern geographical knowledge now precludes the existence of undiscovered terrestrial Utopias, intelligences superior to frail and incompetent man have to be sought for in inter-galactic space. We shall see, too, how these same ideas were powerfully effective among those who rediscovered and reconstructed the Druids from the late seventeenth century onwards.

Another problem presented to us by the classical texts arises from the common practice in antiquity of an author using other written sources, often in lengthy quotation or paraphrase, without acknowledgement. The older scholastic tradition, continuing indeed until the development of modern science, was fundamentally based on an appeal to authority supported by citations from other writers rather than empirically examining the data afresh, and from this developed the unacknowledged use of secondary sources. We shall see how, for instance, in the present enquiry four of the main writers referring to Celtic religion and the Druids appear to derive in great part from a single source, while minor copying, or the transference of some appropriate phrase or epithet from one context to another can also be detected. We must also remember the conventions according to which the books which may contain such references were written in the Greek and Roman world. The basically geographical and ethnographical works from which our soundest evidence comes are nearer to empirical and objective statements than the historical or political works (they are really almost impossible to separate) which were set pieces of rhetoric and literary artifice written to appropriate and accepted patterns, which included edifying and moralizing arrangements of the 'facts', and the introduction of stock figures, invented speeches and conventional situations. And of course, as at all times and in all places, the statements we have to consider are coloured by the 'philosophies' or ideologies of the various individuals or schools of writers.

One set of difficulties is semantic, and applies not only to the classical texts, but to those in the Celtic vernacular still to be considered. Does the very word 'Druid', for instance, have the same meaning in the text of an early Greek geographer, a later Roman historian, and an Irish hero-tale? Or again, what is the significance of an epithet like that usually translated 'most just', when applied by Strabo (or his source, Posidonius) to the Druids as well as to· Moses, Rhadamanthus and the Scythians, but previously used by Herodotus of the Getae and by Homer of the Abioi? One wonders too when a Latin poet uses *fanum* or *delubrum* for a Celtic sanctuary rather than the more usual *templum*, whether this implies some structural difference or whether it is no more than elegant variation in the vocabulary of a self-conscious literary artist. Such questions may not be capable of answer, but they must at least be borne in mind.

THE OLD IRISH TEXTS

The final set of problems in elucidating the ancient Druids is that posed by the old Irish texts referred to earlier. We have already seen that we can obviously use only those texts which present us with a pagan and pre-Christian world when investigating a pagan priesthood, and this necessarily excludes all but the group of old Irish sources already indicated. Here we must remember four main facts. In the first place, they are the products of minds and imaginations infinitely more remote from our own than those of the classical authors, coming as they do from an archaic and barbarian tradition with its roots deep in prehistoric Europe and without any of the self-conscious and analytical element which in the classical civilized tradition helps us to an understanding of it. Secondly, in the form in which they have survived the old Irish tales are early medieval written versions of fragments of an older orally transmitted tradition, already remote and archaic to the scribes and scholars who first brought them into manuscript form. Add to this again the fact that the past to which they belonged was pre-Christian and pagan, whereas the medieval redactors were clerics of the Christian Church which had

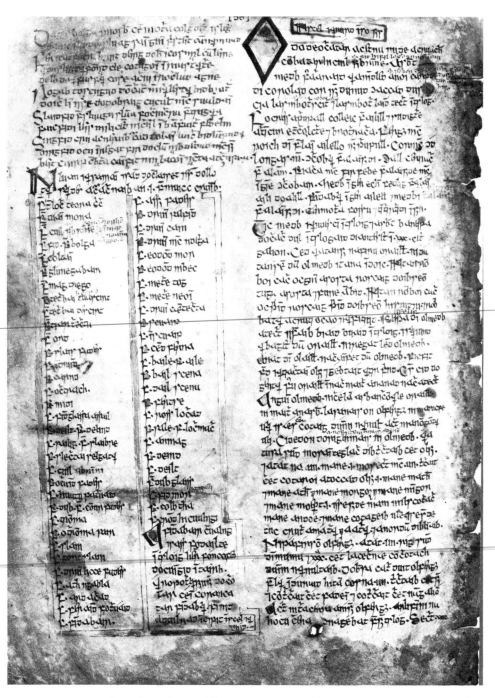

1 Page from the twelfth-century MS *Leabhar na h-Uidhre*, containing the greater part of the *Táin Bó Cúalnge* (The Cattle-Raid of Cooley), the main ancient Irish hero-tale. (Library of the Royal Irish Academy).

stamped out and supplanted the older faiths. National pride and strong antiquarian feelings for lineage and the past of Ireland had to make a compromise with the abominations of heathendom. And finally, there is the fact that they relate exclusively to Ireland, whereas the older *testimonia* refer to parts of continental Europe and to Britain. Ireland was a Celtic outpost beyond the Imperial frontiers, and the archaeological evidence demonstrates that in many ways it was even more distinct from the continental La Tène tradition than was Britain, itself insular and individual enough.

So much for the sources for a knowledge of the ancient Druids, which in the remainder of the book we will examine in detail. Some space has *1* been devoted to setting out the peculiar quality of our different classes of evidence, because almost all discussions of the Druids in non-technical literature have suffered from a failure to appreciate these qualities, and to use the sources sufficiently critically. As a result of this, for three hundred years or so the Druids have appeared in a number of very strange disguises indeed, and these misunderstandings are still with us. We must, however, also concern ourselves with the revival of interest in the priesthood from the seventeenth century onwards, and the circumstances which have brought about the existence of societies calling themselves Druids today, and the popular ideas associated with them. Here the sources are far more straightforward, and abundantly documented, for we move into phases of the history of ideas and the changes in literary and artistic taste which have been well charted. We shall see how the ideas of Primitivism and the Noble Savage were taken up again from their classical origins by scholars whose training in thought and unconscious apprehensions in feeling came in fact from the same Greek and Roman sources. To this were soon to be added elements of increasing fantasy, as the Druids, now standing charismatically within the Stonehenge horseshoe, became a compelling magnet for many a psychological misfit and lonely crank, and we find ourselves in a world of books which, all too frequently, are like that on witchcraft written by the sinister Mr Karswell in M. R. James's ghost story, who 'seemed to put the *Golden Legend* and the *Golden Bough* exactly on a par, and believe both: a pitiable exhibition, in short'.

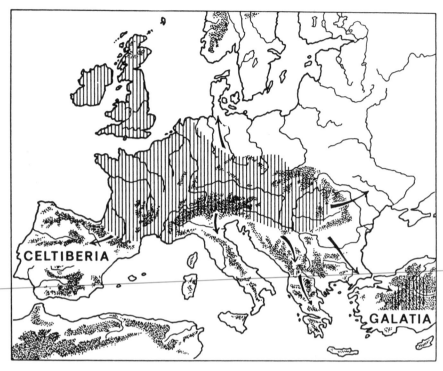

CELTIBERIA

GALATIA

2 The Celtic world at its maximum expansion. The evidence is archaeological, historical and philological. Archaeologically, early La Tène culture is recognizable from *c.* 475 BC in the Rhineland and adjacent areas and by the fourth century in north-east France and by inference probably as early as this in the British Isles. In the Iberian peninsula Celtic elements mingled with those of the Iberians and other indigenous peoples from the fifth century, and Celtic settlement in north Italy seems equally early. In east Europe Celts appear from the beginning of the fourth century and in the early third century historically attested Celtic migrations moved through the Balkans to found the Galatian settlements in Asia Minor.

Chapter Two

THE CELTIC WORLD OF THE DRUIDS

THE SOURCES

The references in the classical authors on which our knowledge of the very existence of the Druids is based range in date from around the end of the third century B C to the fourth century A D, and relate to Western Europe (and almost exclusively to Gaul) and to Britain. The earliest vernacular texts in Old Irish represent written recensions of an oral tradition dating from somewhere shortly before the fifth century A D and relate only to Ireland. We have therefore a virtual continuity over five hundred years so far as actual chronology is concerned, but an abrupt shift of scene between the comments of the Greek and Roman writers and the indigenous Celtic record. Nevertheless all the literary sources are set within a consistent framework which can be historically, linguistically and ethnographically defined as that of the ancient Celts. That this was a unit not only in the sense of sharing a common language, or variant dialects of a single tongue, is shown both by the recognition of the Celts as a 'people' by the classical world (as distinct as, for instance, Scythians or Ethiopians), and by the evidence of common traditions in material culture perceptible to the archaeologist today.

Until 121 B C in Southern France, 58 B C in Gaul beyond that limit, and A D 43 in Britain, this Celtic world, although the subject of comment by literate peoples, was a 'prehistoric' one, not yet historic in the literal sense owing to the lack of written records in communities in which, with very infrequent exceptions, writing was not a social and hardly an individual need. Such communities are therefore basically perceptible only by archaeological means – text-free archaeology – but in part they are illuminated by the comments of the Greek and Roman writers, who provide a highly important text-aided element. It is among these comments that we find those dealing with aspects of Celtic religion, and with those responsible for its maintenance: a priesthood in the widest sense and including that group known as Druids. Ireland, never under Roman rule, and the subject of practically no comment by those concerned with the conquest and Romanization of the British province, has no archaeology aided by classical texts, but instead has its own vernacular literature, the orally transmitted tales of the supernatural and heroic saga committed to writing by early medieval Christian scribes, but with an archaic nucleus relating to circumstances somewhat earlier than the political and religious situation historically known to have obtained in the fifth century A D.

To place the Druids in their proper setting we should then try to form a picture of the Celtic world to which they belonged from text-free and text-aided sources, conveniently centred on the time at which Posidonius, our main literary authority, was flourishing, in the late second and early first centuries B C. For this period, of course, the Irish sources can only be used as a general indication of a state of affairs well before their own time, but in the archaic world of traditional, con-serving, societies, the discrepancy of date is of no great moment, as the close correspondence so often apparent between the classical and ver-nacular literary evidence demonstrates. We shall find straight away indications of a remarkably homogeneous culture perceptible in archaeo-logical material and confirmed and extended by the texts, spread over a very wide area of Europe and extending into Asia Minor; a homo-geneity that had appeared by the third century B C and continued until (and in some degree beyond) the incorporation of large areas of the Celtic world within the Roman Empire. The British Isles share many elements of this common Celtic tradition, but Britain has an indivi-duality distinguishing it from the rest of the Celtic world of the last few centuries B C, and Ireland has its own distinctive features which set it aside from Britain and the Continent, though having links with both.

The distribution of Celtic culture is demonstrated by archaeology, the comments of Greek and Roman geographers and historians, and by Celtic place-names attested by inscriptions and by the classical writers just mentioned, or surviving in post-classical forms. As we shall shortly see, the material culture archaeologically classified as middle or late La Tène shows a striking uniformity in many features – weapon and tool types, fortification techniques, styles of decoration and of ornaments, burial modes – over a surprisingly large area of Europe. From the classical writers we have not only the location of a large number of named tribal groups but knowledge of the movements of the Celts from the time of the raids into Italy at the beginning of the fourth century B C – the marauding war-bands that thrust through the Balkans to Delphi, and eventually established the Galatian settlements in Asia Minor in 279–78 B C are a case in point. Celtic mercenaries served in the Greek forces, as in Sicily in 368 B C and in Egypt in 274. Place-names of tribal centres, or of natural features such as rivers and hills, underline the archaeological evidence and hint of phases of folk-movement, as when the names com-pounded with the element -briga extend to Iberia but not to the British Isles, which however share with Continental Europe those in -magus or -dunum.

In sum, the evidence shows us the Celts as a people originating (in archaeological terms) in Central and West Central Europe, and by the third century B C established from Iberia in the west to the Carpathians and the borders of the Ukraine in the east, with the Galatian colony as a still more easterly outpost. Southwards they reach to the Alps, and march with the civilizations of the classical world. Northwards they take in the British Isles, and find their northern boundary along the southern edge of the Teutonic, Slav and Finno-Ugrian peoples on a line roughly marked by the modern cities of Cologne, Kassel, Leipzig and Cracow. Trade connections extended beyond the Celtic frontier, into the North European Plain and Scandinavia, and into South Russia as far as the Crimea and the Volga. In terms of geographical regions, Celtic Europe was essentially the southern part of the deciduous temperate forest zone, its northern limit still some 700 miles south of the natural extent of the coniferous woodlands, and not far in fact from the eventual boundary of the Roman Empire in Europe under Trajan. The forests of barbarian Europe north of the Alps were a strange and rather ominous reality to the Mediterranean peoples, coming from territories robbed of so much of their natural woodland by the centuries-long devastation of men and goats.

TECHNOLOGY

As our evidence for Celtic culture is basically archaeological, however much the written sources may from time to time give colour and corroboration, it will be convenient in continuing our brief assessment of the background of the Druids, to proceed in terms of the scale of the reliability of inference put forward by Hawkes and referred to in the last chapter. We begin therefore with questions of technology, on which archaeology can inform us in the most direct and reliable manner.

The technological capacities of any people depend in the first place upon their exploitation of raw materials. Out of the vast range of natural resources available to man, however, only those will be selected that are appropriate to the economy and mode of life of a community, those in fact which are socially necessary and acceptable. In an economy which is relatively static in its technology, however well adjusted, a limited range of natural products will continue to be drawn upon generation after generation; in one which has a tradition of practical experiment and invention, new potentialities will be explored and exploited. To a community using stone for edge-tools and ignorant of the principles of metallurgy, deposits of copper, tin or iron ore are not only irrelevant, but do not, so to say, exist in the world-picture of the society in question; to hunters, good farming land is a meaningless concept.

In Europe of the last few centuries BC civilized and barbarian communities alike drew on a common range of natural resources, the degree and efficiency of their exploitation being controlled by the social and industrial competence of the respective peoples. Greeks and Romans, Celts, Scythians and the rest, shared in a stage of technological development in which iron was the normal material for edge-tools and weapons: in the model of the past current since the nineteenth century, all were in an Iron Age. Barbarian Europe beyond the Aegean had been using iron

3 Distribution of iron ingots of 'double-pyramid' form in later Celtic Europe.

since the seventh century BC, obtaining the metal from mined ore or bog deposits, and in the Celtic world at the time of the Druids organizing
3   a regular trade in characteristic double-pointed ingots of metal. It has indeed been suggested that the emergence of the rich Early Celtic culture of the Rhineland as far back as the fifth century BC may have been due to the trading power of native 'iron-masters' exploiting the local ores.

Blacksmithing was an important craft, and not only were tools such as knives or shears or axe-heads made to stock patterns right across the Celtic world, but so were more elaborate pieces of decorative as well as
4, 5   functional ironwork, such as fire-dogs, or chains for hanging the bronze cauldron over an open fire. Iron too was used by armourers for swords, spears and the defensive mountings of wooden shields, but although steel was sometimes produced by adding carbon during the forging process, it does not seem to have been consistently or really deliberately manufactured as such, any more than in the classical civilizations. Copper and tin were in constant demand for bronze-working, the crafts-
6, 7   men turning out cauldrons, bowls, flagons, mirrors, ornaments and even sculpture, as well as the parade equipment of warriors' helmets, sword
8   hilts and scabbards, shield mounts and horse gear. While iron ore is of common occurrence, resources of copper and tin are very restricted, and involved problems of trade and distribution in their exploitation. Gold and silver were also employed for ornaments and objects of display and,

4 Double bull-headed iron fire-dog from Barton, Cambridgeshire. Early first century A D.

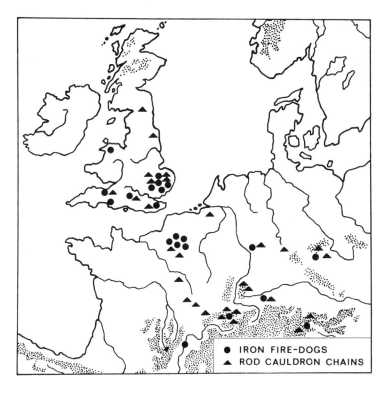

● IRON FIRE-DOGS
▲ ROD CAULDRON CHAINS

5 Map of iron fire-dogs of the type of Ill. 4, and composite rod-and-ring iron chains for suspending a cauldron.

6 *(opposite)* Bronze wine-flagon with enamel and coral inlay from Basse-Yutz, Moselle, late fifth century BC. 7 *(above left)* Terminal boss of bronze shield from River Witham, Lincolnshire, probably second century BC. 8 *(above right)* Central bronze boss of shield, from River Thames at Wandsworth, probably second century BC. 9 *(below)* Massive bronze armlet with enamel inlay, Castle Newe, Aberdeenshire, first-second century AD.

from the second century BC, Celtic coinage in these metals was in circulation. Bronze-work was on occasion decorated with coloured

enamels, a technique probably acquired from the eastern regions of the Caucasus and of the Sarmatian peoples. In matters of technique and technical competence the Celtic metal-workers were not far behind those of Greece and Rome, and were about equal to those of medieval Northern Europe.

From the earth products other than metals could be won, especially salt: this could also be obtained by evaporating the water of inland saline springs, or on the coast from the sea. The inland salt resources of Europe had been exploited for many centuries, and the product was not only a valuable object of trade and exchange in itself, but made possible another marketable commodity, salted and cured meat (especially bacon, for which Gaul was renowned in Roman times), and salt fish. Clay too was of course widely employed for making pottery, either the rough hand-made peasant products of the village or farmstead, or the wheel-turned wares of skilled potters. Baked clay was not however used for bricks or tiles: brick-and-mortar and concrete architecture was an achievement of the Mediterranean world. Suitably gritty stones were widely and universally used for grinding corn in rotary hand-mills in every household: the technological improvement of employing rotary rather than to-and-fro movement had been achieved in the barbarian world at least by the second century BC, even in Britain. Stone was used for the building of house walls and defences, usually as undressed blocks and always without mortar, throughout those areas where stone occurred.

AGRICULTURE AND ECONOMY

Plants and animals provided both food and other products in either wild or domesticated form. The basic cereal crops of prehistoric Europe since the sixth millennium BC had been wheat and barley, and to these had been added oats and rye as these species, resistant to cold and wet climatic conditions, developed from wild grasses which had been weeds of cultivation in the original mixed crops. Leguminous vegetables such as peas and beans were cultivated, and quantities of wild seeds seem to have been collected and eaten in the form of gruel or porridge, and of course nuts and fruit, either wild or slightly improved by cultivation, like apples, were freely available. The largely uncleared forests provided an endless supply of timber for buildings and fortifications and for all the products of carpenters, coopers, wheelwrights and boat-builders, as well as the material for hurdling and wattle-and-daub construction. Straw and reeds provided material for thatch or bedding and, with other species such as heather, ropes; flax and nettle fibres provided textiles. As with most peasant peoples one can assume a large body of traditional medicine lying behind the few specific references in the classical writers to herbs used by the Celtic priesthood. Cereals were also used for brewing various kinds of beer: wine however was imported from the Mediterranean world as a luxury drink.

Domestic animals comprised cattle, sheep, goats, pigs and the horse (a pony rather, not more than about 10–11 hands high). Wild animals available for hunting included cattle (the Urus or Aurochs), Red Deer and Roe Deer and in southern Europe at least the Fallow Deer; bears, boars and a wide range of birds. River, lake and sea fish, together with seals and cretaceans, afforded a complementary harvest of the waters. Together they formed a group of natural resources for not only immediate (or in smoked, cured or salted form, long-term) food supplies of meat, fish, milk and cheese, but also stocks of leather, horn, skins, furs, rawhide rope, feathers for arrows or adornment, bone and antler and ivory for the craftsman, wool for textiles and manure for agriculture. Bees, wild and almost certainly domesticated as well, provided honey for sweetening and for mead, as well as wax, needed especially for *cire perdue* metal-casting.

11

In short, the natural resources available to and utilized by the Celtic peoples were almost exactly those of the earlier Middle Ages of northwestern Europe, and in their exploitation there was similarly little significant disparity. The economy which these commodities supported was throughout the Celtic world based on mixed farming, with cereal crops and livestock, at a very competent peasant level. The basic structure of such a farming economy had been in existence in prehistoric Europe for five thousand years in the south and east, and nearly four thousand in the north and west. The traction plough, rather than the primitive hoe or digging-stick, had been employed in Britain since the third, and in northern Europe from early in the second millennium B C, and roughly rectangular field-systems can be dated in Britain to the middle of the millennium and some may be earlier: by the last few centuries before the Roman Conquest they are recognizably widespread in southern England.

In the British Isles there are indications that in some areas (north and west Britain, and in Ireland) the economy of the early Celtic Iron Age may have been based more particularly on pastoralism, with wealth centred in large flocks and herds, rather than on intensive corn-growing in conjunction with some form of animal husbandry, and the classical sources imply an element of pastoral nomadism in some areas of Europe, notably among the Germani. But in the areas of intensive Celtic agriculture some system of fallow, rotation or manuring had clearly been evolved to obviate rapid land exhaustion and the consequent shift of settlements at frequent intervals.

The unit of settlement was normally, on the European continent, the village, but in the British Isles the individual farmstead or croft appears to be more frequent. Buildings were usually of wood, exceptionally of unmortared stone, and thatched, loosely scattered about the settlement area in a tradition going back to the earliest farming communities of Europe and contrasting with the closely packed agglomeration of the Mediterranean village or town. In Gaul by the time of Caesar's conquest there had clearly been a development of the social unit towards a rustic attempt at the classical concept of townships in some of the *oppida*

10 Gold stater of Philip II of Macedon (fourth century BC) and Celtic copies from the tribe of the Bellovaci and from southern England (first century BC), showing the transmutation of a classical into a Celtic art style.

11 Bronze figure of a boar, from Hounslow, first centuries BC/AD. The boar was not only an important item in Celtic diet, but played a part in religion and mythology.

or tribal capitals, as at Bibracte 'with winding streets and houses vaguely suggesting Mediterranean house-plans but with architectural possibilities limited by the absence of mortar'. Houses were, over the greater part of Europe, rectangular and usually single-roomed or with minor divisions; in Iberia alternatively and in the British Isles universally, circular: circular houses must have also existed in Gaul. Settlements or farmsteads were either unenclosed or undefended, or within palisades or earthwork or stone defences of varying magnitude, from a light fence to a massive fortification.

Fortifications, on hill-tops or in flat country, are an insistent, melancholy and recurrent feature of the Celtic world, and while they obviously bespeak a situation of raiding and warfare among small political units – a state of affairs confirmed by the literary evidence, classical and vernacular – they pose many problems of social organization in their building and their manning, their status among other settlements and farmsteads, and their relation to political power centred in tribes or individuals known from historical evidence. Some certainly, especially in Gaulish and adjacent territory, can be reasonably interpreted as permanently occupied tribal capitals or *oppida*, as at Bibracte, a capital of the tribe of the Aedui, Alesia of the Mandubii, or Manching, of the Vindelici.

12, 13

14

35

12 The hill-fort of Maiden Castle, Dorset, showing earlier fort of *c.* 300 BC later enlarged with multiple ramparts and elaborate gateways, *c.* 100 BC in their final form.

13 The medieval cathedral city of Old Sarum, Wiltshire, with Norman castle and cathedral, abandoned *c.* 1220 AD. The medieval earthworks surrounding the site incorporate the ramparts of an Iron Age hill-fort.

14 The site of the Gaulish *oppidum* at Alesia, held by Vercingetorix against Julius Caesar in 52 BC.

15, 16, 17 Three coins issued by Julius Caesar to commemorate his Gaulish victories, showing an elephant trampling on the serpent of Gaul, a trophy with a seated figure probably of Vercingetorix, and a warrior in a chariot.

15   Other aspects of Celtic warfare are reflected in the equipment known from archaeological remains or later representations in classical sculpture
16   – swords, spears, shields and sporadically body-armour and helmets – and also of chariots, known from similar sources, and the literature.
17   Celtic chariotry had ultimately oriental roots, and was an integral part of warfare in such documented engagements as that of Sentinum (295 BC) or Clastidium (222) and among the Arverni (121). Posidonius,
18   writing mainly of the second century BC, describes chariot warfare as a Gaulish practice, but by Caesar's time, from 58 BC onwards, it had been given up in the continental territories with which he was concerned, probably as a result of the Celts trying to adopt defensive measures more in accordance with Roman techniques of war. Caesar was however to encounter it (to his surprise) in southern Britain in 56 BC, and it survived in Caledonia into the third century AD, forming also the characteristic background of the early Irish hero-tales of later date.

18 Roman coins concerned with Celtic warfare: head of Vercingetorix; naked
warrior in chariot with shield and spear; trophies including Celtic shield, horned
helmet and animal-headed trumpet or carnyx; a head of Gallia with a carnyx, and
crossed carnices, shield and wheel.

Within this framework of warfare, conducted on a petty scale between families, clans, tribes or coalitions, and in a manner which was to survive in the Scottish Highlands to the middle of the eighteenth century, fit the practices of individual combat, ritual nakedness in battle, head-hunting, battle-cries and chants, and the rest of the excitements dear to the simple heart of the hero. It is a ruder, more rough-and-tumble world than that of most surviving epic poetry, even if in all of this the bard heavily gilds an unprepossessing scene where blood and rust erode the cruel iron.

We have then a barbaric society, with an economic background based on plough-agriculture and pastoralism in varying degrees of dominance in the various parts of the Celtic world. The stratified social structure which we find documented by the classical and vernacular texts is reflected archaeologically in the presence not only of princely burials with rich offerings accompanying the dead, but by an aristocratic art of the adornment of warriors, their women, their horses and chariots, decorated in an interlocking and developing series of traditions all united within what has rightly been called one of the great unclassical arts of Europe. Inference from the archaeological evidence suggests that this is a pattern of society going back in barbarian Europe to at least the middle of the second millennium BC: we are looking at an Heroic Age, akin on the one hand to that of Homer or the Rig-Veda, and on the other to Beowulf and the Sagas; behind it and supporting it is a world very close to that of Hesiod's *Works and Days*.

The structure of Celtic society must be considered in more detail shortly: we are in Hawkes's second stage of legitimate inference from text-free archaeology, that of subsistence-economics, although we have used a little corroborative material from literate sources. As we saw, in the old, three-ages, model of prehistory, the Celts are in the Iron Age, using this metal for edge-tools and weapons, as did their classical contemporaries and their medieval successors. What is more to the point is that archaeology alone, without the texts, in the rustic farmsteads and peasant hamlets; the forts and strongholds of chieftains and tribes; the barbaric panoply of parade and war; even (as we shall see) the evidence for rituals including human sacrifice and head-hunting, shows us a picture of a society barbarous and uncivilized in its essentials, however much superficial veneer may have been acquired by exceptional individuals and societies in for instance Gaul. And that we have read the archaeological evidence correctly, the texts amply confirm.

An iron-using, barbarian, economy then, based on its flocks and herds and its ploughlands, with a warrior-aristocracy supporting skilled artists and craftsmen, and also surely an underworld of horse-breeders and horse-copers for the highly trained chariot ponies. A self-supporting economy, but with enough surplus to trade with the civilized world, especially for wine and luxury goods. Some sort of a merchant class may well have emerged, particularly in Gaul. A world of gross meat-eaters, contrary to Mediterranean traditions, feasting round an open hearth 'in a cleanly but leonine fashion, raising up whole limbs in both hands and biting off the meat', with fire-dogs and roasting spits, great cauldrons hung on elaborate chains, and a preference for boiled pork; drinking home-made beer or mead, or swallowing their imported wine neat, rather than diluted as a decent Greek or Roman would prefer. Their architectural performance was limited to building in timber and wattle-and-daub, or rough stone in the north, in straggling settlements or single farms set in assarts and clearings among the ever-encompassing forests. With the invaluable aid of the literary sources we can go further and perceive something unattainable by purely archaeological means, the social structure of the Celtic world, its language and literature, and finally something of the ritual, magic and religious beliefs among which the Druids take their immediate place.

THE SOCIAL ORDER

The two main areas of the Celtic world significant in our enquiry into the Druids, Gaul and Ireland, both provide evidence for the Celtic social order, which can be seen to have been essentially the same in both regions. The Irish vernacular sources show us a simpler and more rustic world than do the classical writers, particularly Caesar, describing Gaul, and this is consonant with the archaeological evidence for a higher degree of sophistication and technological achievement on the Continent. The major social units in Gaul were what are usually translated 'tribes' – *ethne* in the Greek and *civitates* in the Roman writers – and these have specific names, the familiar Helvetii or Veneti, Aedui or Atrebates. Within these large tribal areas there would be *pagi*, smaller territorial or kinship units or 'clans', and in Caesar's time there were impermanent and shifting political coalitions in which the more powerful tribes might have several others in a relation of client powers. By this time too what had been an original system of tribal chieftainships (or 'kings') was being replaced by an annually elected magistracy in the Roman manner (a member of which was known as a *vergobretos*), or by the oligarchic rule of the council of elders originally responsible to the 'king' (*rix*) whose position had to some extent at least been elective from within the choice presented by the dynastic families, and there had also been a separate war leader on occasion. A phrase in Tacitus suggests that a similar decline in chieftainship had taken place in Britain. Caesar records eleven Gaulish 'kings': two had ceased to reign by his time, and three he himself set up. We should not be misled by this grandiloquent translation of the Latin *rex* or the Gaulish *rix*: most were 'no more than petty invading chieftains whose lives were spent in marauding one another's territory and preying on their subject peoples'. The documentary evidence from Britain shows, in the intimidating personalities of Boudica and of Cartimandua, that women could be elected to the status of tribal 'queens', and archaeo- *19, 20* logical corroboration is given by richly furnished women's graves. Below the king and the royal family, society in Gaul was tripartite, with two classes of landowning freemen, the knights or barons (*equites*) from whom the council of elders was chosen, and the priesthood or clerisy,

19 Bronze mirror with engraved back from an aristocratic woman's grave at Birdlip, Gloucestershire; early first century AD.

20 Bronze mirror with engraved back from Desborough, Northamptonshire. Mirrors such as this and that from Birdlip (Ill. 19) represent a distinctive type produced by Celtic craftsmen in Britain in the last decades of the pre-Roman period. Fifteen are known in this country and one found its way as an export to the Low Countries to be buried in a Roman grave at Nijmagen. They seem to be made by more than one master craftsman in south-west Britain. Their size and beauty emphasize the status of the women who used them; their weight suggests they were held up by a ladies' maid.

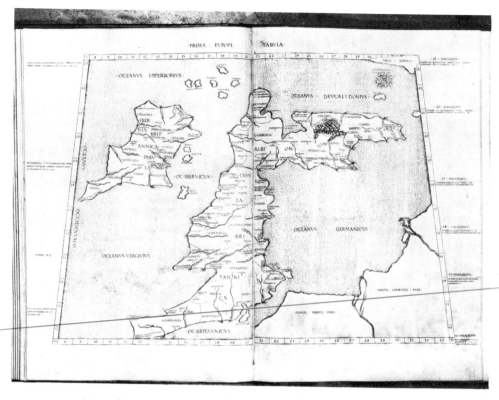

21 Map of the British Isles drawn from Ptolemy's latitude and longitude lists of the second century AD. Note the distortions especially of Scotland by 90°, arising from discrepancies caused by a clash between the terrestrial and astronomical data available to him.

including *druides*. This learned class comprised not only Druids, but bards (*bardoi*), and seers or diviners (*vates* or *manteis*), and probably other un-named functionaries. Below these representatives of church and state came the unfree and landless men, the *plebes*. There was an internal grading in power and position among the 'knights', and it seems that they did not constitute a closed caste, and some social mobility seems to have been possible. The Druid and allied religious élite was equally not a caste, but open to entry from outside, from the class of *equites*.

The evidence from the law-tracts and hero-tales in Archaic Irish, which represent the earliest literary stratum, shows that the normal area of the tribe (*túath*) ruled by a 'king' (*rí*) was not comparable with the Gaulish *civitas*, but with the *pagus*. The nearest approach to *civitates* would have been the five sub-kingdoms or provinces (Ulster or Connacht for instance) each under a provincial 'king' and comprising a group of *túath* units: Ulster, to take an example, contained 35. The geographical information assembled by Ptolemy in the early second century BC contained the names of twenty 'tribes' in Ireland (comparable with the 33 for Britain), and our vernacular sources clearly do not relate to this situation, but to a later state of affairs, as collateral evidence implies. In

21

44

Britain, incidentally, there are hints of *pagi* as sub-divisions formerly existing within some of the big tribal areas and later absorbed into them: the *civitas* was ruled by a 'king', or exceptionally a 'queen'.

On a lower and more primitive scale, 'kingship' was universal in Ireland, elective from within the dynasty. Below the king came the land-owning 'grades of nobility' – the Gaulish *equites* – and between them and the freemen commoners came those of exceptional gifts of skill, the *aes dána* or 'men of art'; expert craftsmen in things, word and thought, blacksmiths and bronze-workers, lawyers and genealogists, poets and musicians. In the Irish scheme of things Druids designated as such are not normally in the dominant position the Gaulish (or at least Caesar's) evidence implies, but are contained within the men of art who were the men of learning, and also included the *filid* who were at once seers and wise men, and the repositories of the oral traditions not only of myth, legend, and family history, but of the formalized language and techniques of prosody in which these were preserved and transmitted, and the jurists responsible for customary law. There was a council of nobles, and a general assembly of the freemen of the tribe: such assemblies merged with the periodic 'fairs', where old and new laws were recited and pro-clamations made, poems declaimed, and sports including horse-racing took place, as well as a market. These open-air gatherings, appropriate to a rustic society without literacy or towns, seem often to have been held at ancient tumulus-cemeteries or similar sacred sites. The annual meeting of the Gaulish Druids in the tribal area of the Carnutes was presumably akin to these provincial gatherings, as would have been the meetings of the Galatian tribes at the sanctuary of Drunemeton in Asia Minor.

There is some evidence in the Irish vernacular sources that the 'men of art' – and particularly, what is for our purpose more important, the learned men who were a constituent of this social group – were itinerant and inter-tribal. 'There was one class of persons which could travel freely,' Professor David Greene has said. 'The literary class . . . by virtue of its sacred office, could pass freely through the iron curtain which separated the tribes from one another. I think it is not going too far to conclude that this privilege extended to all members of that sacred class which was known to the Gauls as *druides* and under varying names in ancient Ireland: they were the *aes dána*, the men of special gifts. . . . The importance of this learned professional class in early Ireland cannot be over-estimated, for, in the absence of towns or any centralized political system, they were the only national institution.' They were to hold this position in Irish society until the sixteenth century, when savage attempts to exterminate these dangerously mobile repositories of native sentiment and lore were made by the Elizabethan English. As we shall see, the Druids were to be placed in a comparable position in Gaul and Britain with the imposition of Roman rule.

We see then a common pattern of society well documented in Gaul and Ireland, and by inference present elsewhere in the Celtic world. Ireland shows it in its simple, rural, form; Gaul by the time of Caesar's campaigns, under influence from the Mediterranean world, was moving towards a more sophisticated type of society with the disappearance of the kingship and the growth of something approaching urban communities in the *oppida* or defended centres of political power, in *civitas* or *pagus*, and a magistracy copying Roman exemplars. Basically it was a social pattern found in Old World antiquity in many contexts, but never, even in its final Celtic form, capable of enlargement beyond the bounds of the *civitas* at best. It was an heroic society with a warrior élite, and for such, raids and wars between tribes, clans, septs or families provide the only means whereby the aristocratic values can be demonstrated and prestige maintained. In itself it was incompatible with civilized government.

LANGUAGE AND LITERACY

Linguistically, we move within a group of closely related Indo-European languages. From a Common Celtic stock differentiation had taken place, at a date unknown but well before the Druids first receive mention, into two main groups, one (Q-Celtic) retaining the original Indo-European 'Q' sound while the other modified it into 'P' (P-Celtic). The Irish of our sources belongs to the archaic and conserving Q-Celtic group; Continental language was the P-Celtic Gallo-Brittonic, represented mainly by Gaulish, with an insular version in British. For Ireland we have abundant evidence for an unwritten oral tradition for the conservation and transmission of poetry, epic, genealogy, anecdote, law and custom, and this can be assumed to have existed throughout the Celtic world. For Gaul indeed we have the specific statement by Caesar that a large body of traditional lore in verse form was deliberately learnt by pupils from their masters, who were in fact the Druids; other classical references to the poems and songs, eulogies and satires of the recognized professional class of bards already mentioned show us that we are in a world very closely akin to that portrayed in the literature reflecting the earliest Irish tradition.

Though writing was not used for imaginative or traditional literature, a state of conditional literacy intermittently existed among the Gaulish upper classes before the Roman conquest: we saw in chapter 1 how restricted the use of writing in a society can be. The long story of Greek trade relations with barbarian western Europe, going back to the seventh century BC, must have included not only the tangible imports of fine bronzes or painted vases, but contributions to the intellectual life of persons remote from Massalia. We shall see how some elements of Greek mathematics and astronomical computations may have entered the Celtic world in this way, and will have to consider the question of the interchange of ideas in rudimentary metaphysics and theoretical speculations.

At all events, Greek letters seem to have been occasionally used for writing among the Celts: an iron sword of the first century BC from

46

22 Coin of the British ruler Addedomaros, showing crossed 'D' to indicate the phonetic value of the dental, as pronounced in Gallo-Brittonic.

Switzerland has a Celtic name – *Korisios* – stamped on it in Greek characters. Caesar has some admittedly rather ambiguous statements that imply however that some knowledge of the Greek alphabet was current among the Gaulish men of learning, and we have noted the South Gaulish inscriptions in Greek characters. At least one Greek usage came to be a 'Gallo-Latin spelling habit' in Jackson's words, in which a Latin X was used as a Greek χ (or X itself was used) to indicate the Celtic *ch* sound (as in the Scottish *loch*), particularly when this was followed by a *t*. This is known in inscriptions from Gaul (TIOCOBREXTIO on the Coligny Calendar discussed later on) and in Britain (ANEXTIOMARO   *23* in an inscription from South Shields), and it also appears earlier as a variant spelling on some coins of the British 'king' Tasciovanus TAXCIAV [ANOS]), of c. 20 BC to AD 10. These usages suggest deliberate modification of the Roman alphabet by the Celtic *literati*, in order to accommodate phonetic values existing in Celtic but not in Latin. Further evidence of this is provided by other orthographic innovations including the barred D (Ð or ÐÐ), the barred SS (S̄S̄), or the use of the Greek θ to represent a group of related sounds also rendered by *ss*. The name AÐÐEDOMAROS was current in Gaul and Britain,   *22* where a 'king' of that name ruled from c. 15 to 1 BC, and ANTE-ÐRIG[OS] struck coins in the early first century BC. The sound involved may be that referred to by Latin writers as the *tau gallicum*, and at all events more than one written convention was devised to express it: it has been remarked that the variation 'implies that occasionally the alphabets used were richer than the phonemic systems of the Celtic dialects they recorded'. Such examples show a scholarly concern for standards of literacy in the Celtic world of learning that contained the Druids, comparable with the calendrical expertise of the Coligny tables discussed in the next chapter and again probably due to long-standing contacts with the Mediterranean world. It has recently been pointed out that there is presumptive evidence for the importation of papyrus as a writing material into Britain between the invasions of Caesar and of Claudius. This clearly would imply conditional literacy among a learned or merchant class, as do the coin inscriptions themselves, and the pre-Conquest graffiti in Roman letters on pottery at Camulodunum (Colchester).

The early Irish world as presented in the earliest vernacular stratum is a wholly illiterate one, though with a compensatory elaboration of the techniques of oral transmission, and the adoption in Ireland, from perhaps the late fourth century AD of an inscriptional alphabet, *Ogam*, probably itself derived from Latin characters, does not concern us here.

THE ARCHAEOLOGY OF CELTIC RELIGION

We may now turn to the last and most difficult stage of archaeological interpretation, the correlation of material remains with the religious activities of the Celts. We saw in the first chapter something of the problems of making any meaningful inference on religious activity from archaeological evidence alone, and we need not go over this again. Although we have literary evidence which will be more fully considered in the next chapter, it does not necessarily illuminate the archaeology. Not only may it be impossible to bring Diogenes and his tub together, or the Druid as known from the texts with the sanctuary identified by archaeology, but that other difficulty of inference, the interpretation of a structure in terms of function, confronts us recurrently. Even if one is reasonably certain in interpreting a structure as a temple or a shrine, or in inferring ritual from burial practices, one cannot then relate them to the beliefs held by the ministrants, nor the Order of the Office.

With these reservations in mind we may go on to some general points. The concept of the temple as an architectural civic monument, ancient in the Mediterranean and even older in the Near East, was as alien to the Celts as to their predecessors in barbarian Europe. We shall see that there are exceptions, mostly attributable to classical influence, but the archaeological evidence is here consonant with the texts in general. Sanctuaries in woodland clearings that might at most be ceremonial enclosures struck the Greek and Roman writers as something unusual, as did the heavy forests themselves. It looks as if much of the awe and horror expressed at the dim barbarian groves may have been inspired by the contrast between a rural continental world in which uncleared woodland still dominated the landscape, and the urban pattern of life in what were by then the increasingly open coastlands of the Mediterranean. In the Germanic world, as Koebner put it, 'the heart of the forest was the seat of the Godhead: there it displayed its awe; there it claimed sacrifice and humble submission. . . . Among the Alemanni, as late as the eighth century, Abbot Pirmin denounced those rites of prayer and magic which propitiated the secret powers of the forest depths and the forest soil.' The forests went on to inspire awe in the townsmen of the Middle Ages – here the pagans lurked, and worse: wild and hairy men, *pilosi* and wood-

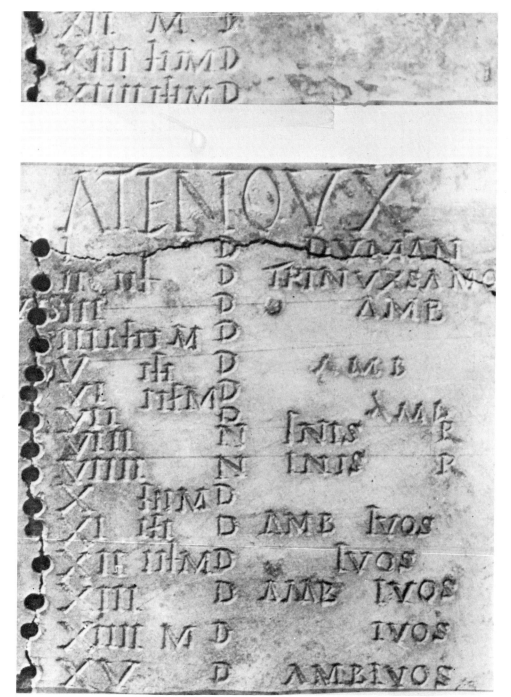

23 Part of the bronze plate engraved with a Gaulish calendar, of the late first century AD, from Coligny near Bourg-en-Bresse (Ain). The language is Gaulish, and the holes down the side are for movable pegs to mark the days. The word ATENOVX ('returning night') marks the division of the month into a 'bright' half and a 'dark' half.

24 Reconstruction of the elements of the destroyed Celtic sanctuary of
Roquepertuse, Bouches-du-Rhône, showing stone pillars with niches containing
human skulls surmounted by a bird figure (?goose) and statues of squatting human
figures. The architecture and sculpture was all originally painted. Third–second
century BC.

25 Stone pillar with carvings of severed human heads re-used as a threshold and (beyond) stone with carved head flanked by skull-niches. Entremont, Provence, before 123 BC.

woses; Hell was well known to be 'surrounded by very thick woods', as an eleventh century poem puts it, and Dante placed *la dolorosa selva* in his Inferno. It is not surprising if a Greek or Roman citizen felt ill at ease in the Celtic jungle.

SHRINES AND TEMPLES

The exceptions to the general pattern, which as we shall see was one of enclosed sanctuary areas and small timber shrines, are found, hardly surprisingly, in the area of southern Gaul conquered as a Roman province in 121 BC. At two sites, Mouriés (Bouches-du-Rhône) and Saint-Blaise (Alpes-Maritimes), fragments of earlier stone-built shrines had been incorporated into Gallo-Greek structures of the fourth century BC: at the former, stelae and a lintel were decorated with stylized figures of horses and riders in a convention that could be earlier than the fifth century, and at the latter was a jamb-stone with niches cut in it which, from the evidence of other sites, would have held skulls or severed heads. At Roquepertuse (Bouches-du-Rhône) such a sanctuary stood at the top of a flight of five steps, with lintels supported on pillars with skull-niches and surmounted by a large sculptured bird, and contained life-size statues of squatting figures – a posture consonant with the Celtic mode of sitting noted by Posidonius and portrayed on other Celtic and Romano-Celtic monuments. There are again a lintel and pillars with skull-niches at Glanum, St-Rémy-en-Provence, associated with a cave and a spring, and re-used in the second century BC. In the *oppidum* of the Saluvii at

24

26 The cult of the severed head; human skull and skeleton set in the hill-fort wall of L'Impernal, Luzech, second century BC.

25 Entremont, Provence, was a remarkable sanctuary, its threshold a re-used pillar carved with stylized human heads, and containing fifteen human skulls of adult men, some cut from dried bodies and some retaining the large iron nails with which they had been fixed to some wooden structure: the place was sacked in 123 BC and these, and the remains of a series of large stone sculptures of warriors and other motifs including severed heads, must date from before this time. Monumental stone sculpture going back to the sixth century BC is known sporadically in the Celtic world (e.g. the Hirschlanden warrior from near Stuttgart) and recurs in later contexts in the Rhineland. The cult of the head and skull is 26 attested by other finds, some from hill-forts in both Gaul and Britain, and by the classical authorities: it is however curious that such dramatic barbarian shrines, under twenty miles from Massalia, escaped comment.

Literary references to any form of a building in a Celtic religious context are in fact very rare. Instances include a mention in Diodorus Siculus of 'temples and sanctuaries', or 'shrines and sacral enclosures', according to one's translation of the Greek; and Suetonius writes of 'fanes and temples' plundered by Caesar in Gaul. Caesar's sword was hung up by the Averni in a temple, according to Plutarch, and the body of Postumius was taken by the Boii to their 'most revered temple', there to be decapitated, and a gold-mounted cup made from the skull, as recounted by Livy and referred to by Silius Italicus. Polybius refers to a temple of Athena in the territory of the Insubrii. Unfortunately we do not know whether we are dealing with more or less factual statements, or with such words as *templum* or *fanum* used as literary terms without regard to architectural truth, and so not necessarily denoting a roofed building.

But Posidonius describes the Celtic priestesses of an island shrine off the mouth of the Loire who ritually stripped the roof from their temple, and re-thatched it, each year, which sounds unambiguous. Posidonius also relates that the Gaulish chieftain Lovernios (in the third century BC) 'made a square enclosure' of vast size within which a suitably lavish feast was held: here there may be some connection with the large rectangular sanctuary enclosures which we shall shortly consider. The much discussed circular temple of Apollo among the Hyperboreans, described in the fourth century BC by Hecateus of Abdera as quoted by Diodorus, is fortunately not our immediate concern, though we must later investigate the Hyperboreans themselves.

Perhaps the best representative of a timber-built temple or shrine of pre-Roman Celtic date is that excavated under London Airport at Heath Row. Within a large quadrangular earthwork enclosure about 450 feet each way were found the bedding-trenches of eleven circular timber houses and much evidence of occupation probably in the main of the fourth century BC. Set away from these houses was a rectangular building represented by the post-holes and bedding-trenches of a massive timber structure, consisting of a central nearly square building 18 by 15 feet, and a surrounding colonnade about 36 by 30 feet. A double-square plan is characteristic of a well-known series of brick and masonry temples of Roman date, widely known in Britain and the Continent, and by reason of their distribution classed as Romano-Celtic, and although the rect-

30, 31

27

40

27 Air photograph of Romano-Celtic double-square temple of mid-second century AD within a pre-Roman square ditched *temenos*, Gosbecks, Colchester, Essex.

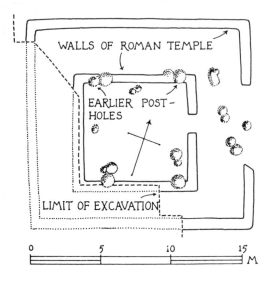

WALLS OF ROMAN TEMPLE

EARLIER POST-
HOLES

LIMIT OF EXCAVATION

0   5   10   15
M

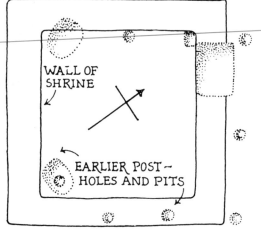

WALL OF
SHRINE

EARLIER POST-
HOLES AND PITS

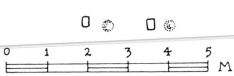

0   1   2   3   4   5
M

28, 29 Post-holes and pits beneath and earlier than square Romano-Celtic masonry temples or shrines at St Germain-les-Rocheux and Schleidweiler, indicating timber buildings in the indigenous Celtic mode which may be pre-Roman and represent native sanctuary sites.

angular proportions of the Heath Row building made its excavator look for Greek prototypes, the Roman series also played their part in the interpretation of the structure as a temple at all. A Romano-Celtic

28 temple at St-Germain-les-Rocheux (Côte d'Or) overlaid the post-holes of its earlier, perhaps Celtic, predecessor, with a central square about the same size as at Heath Row, and there seem to have been pre-Roman posts under the similar Romano-Celtic temple at Worth in Kent, and

29 an early post-structure under a Roman shrine at Schleidweiler near Trier. Such a sequence may not have been uncommon, and Harlow in Essex and Woodeaton in Oxfordshire are among presumptive sites.

30, 31 During the making of London Airport at Heath Row, Middlesex, a rescue excavation revealed a ditched enclosure containing circular timber-built houses and one rectangular building which is best interpreted as a temple. The site dates probably from the fourth century BC.

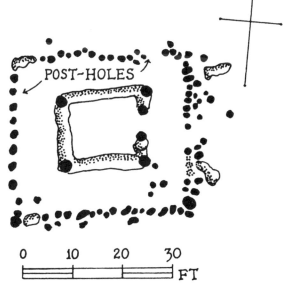

POST-HOLES

0   10   20   30
FT

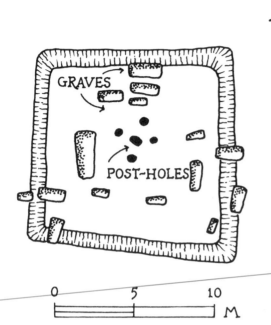

GRAVES

POST-HOLES

0   5   10   M

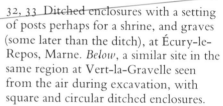

32, 33 Ditched enclosures with a setting of posts perhaps for a shrine, and graves (some later than the ditch), at Écury-le-Repos, Marne. *Below*, a similar site in the same region at Vert-la-Gravelle seen from the air during excavation, with square and circular ditched enclosures.

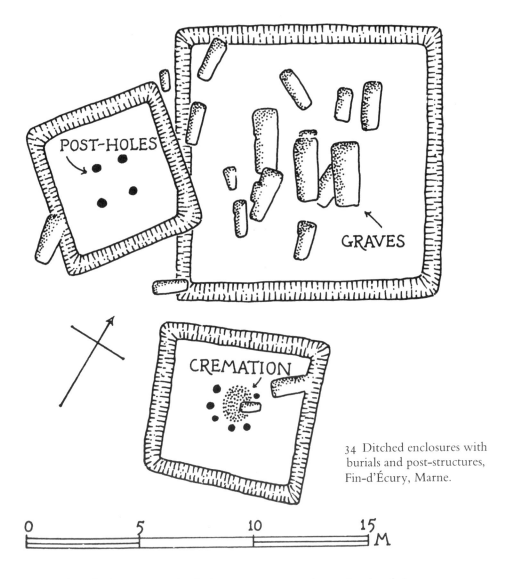

POST-HOLES

GRAVES

CREMATION

34 Ditched enclosures with burials and post-structures, Fin-d'Écury, Marne.

0   5   10   15 M

A series of what seem to be little square or sometimes circular shrines are represented by post-holes within small square earthwork enclosures associated with pre-Roman Celtic cemeteries in the Marne. These *32, 33, 34* timber shrines may be no more than five feet across, and may be compared with similar settings of four posts, from about five to eight feet square, interpreted as Iron Age shrines in the Netherlands, where they may have origins in earlier structures going back into the second millennium BC.

The interpretation of these simple four-post structures as Celtic shrines raises an interesting problem in interpretation when we turn to Iron Age Britain, where similar post-groups in settlement sites have normally been explained as granaries set on stilts. But here one wonders whether alternative explanations in terms of shrines might not sometimes be

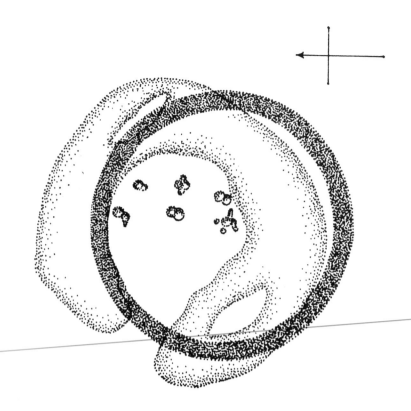

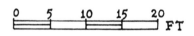

0   5   10   15   20 **FT**

35 Circular Romano-Celtic shrine overlying a
pre-Roman enclosure with wide ditch and
post-setting, at Frilford, Berkshire.

equally apposite, though equally incapable of logical proof: the eight-
foot-square post-setting immediately to the west of the Romano-Celtic
temple at Maiden Castle, Dorset, with a hearth inside, is a case in point,
as is a similar setting, with hearth and native pottery, at Marnhull, also
in Dorset. Here there is a curious structure nearby of Roman date, with
a bedding-trench 17 by 13 feet, interpreted as a house but perhaps again
ritual rather than domestic. We are more happy in our interpretation
when we turn to the small square, circular or semicircular post structures
which antedate the Roman stone buildings in the famous Temple
Precinct at Trier, and must be their Celtic predecessors: not far away, at
Ruckweiler, circular, semicircular and oval post-settings were associated
with a late pre-Roman Celtic cemetery. At St Margarethen am Silber-
berg, the *oppidum* of the Norici, a roughly circular post structure some
15 feet across has also been claimed as a shrine.

35   At Frilford (Berks), again antedating a Romano-Celtic double-square
temple, was a circular post-enclosure, and a shrine within a broad
penannular ditch with post-holes likely to have held ritual rather than

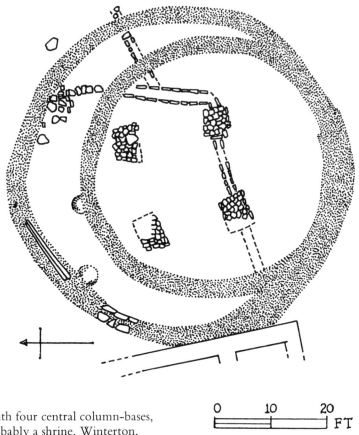

36 Circular building with four central column-bases, Romano-Celtic and probably a shrine, Winterton, Lincolnshire.

0 10 20 FT

structural uprights, with a votive deposit of a ploughshare, model sword and model shield. At Maiden Castle a circular Iron Age structure ante-dated an oval Roman temple. The circular Roman temple in Celtic territory in Gaul or Britain seems probably to reflect native prototypes, built in timber or delimited by ditches or other means as open sanctuaries. Recent excavations in Collyweston Great Wood, Northants., revealed a complex of Romano-British shrines, some octagonal or hexagonal but others circular in plan and not all necessarily roofed structures. A few miles away, at Brigstock, were a polygonal and a circular shrine of third–fourth century AD date, the former overlying a penannular ditch, pre-sumptively pre-Roman, and the latter apparently connected with some Romano-Celtic horse-and-rider cult. At Winterton in Lincolnshire a circular building of the early second century AD with four central column-bases has been interpreted by the excavator as a house of tradi-tional native plan built in a Roman idiom, but here again a shrine would be a possible alternative. There may be many such sites with pre-Roman origins, although in the circular shrine at Thistleton in Rutland the first–

36

37

59

phase wooden building, later replaced in masonry, was no earlier than the early first century AD. Some very curious native survival seems implicit in the Roman cremation burials of the early second century AD, surrounded by rings of close-set wooden posts in bedding-trenches, on Overton Down in Wiltshire, and in comparable sites in the Netherlands. A particularly interesting example of a native temple-type in Britain which, however, is almost certainly not Celtic but Germanic, is the
38 circular shrine near Housesteads on Hadrian's Wall. Roughly built and only 17 feet in diameter, it dates from the early third century and its attribution rests on the finding of a massive stone door-head and inscribed jamb, and two altars, all with dedications by German units of
39 the Roman Army. The larger altar is dedicated to Mars Thincsus and his consorts the Alaisiagae, a popular Teutonic triad.

Interpretation of function, as we have seen, can at times be somewhat insecurely based, and, in passing, a final possibility of an alternative reading of the evidence may be suggested in the seventh–sixth century BC site of the Goldberg in southern Germany. Here a large settlement of rectangular wooden buildings – houses, barns, sheds – was excavated, and in one corner, set apart from these and within a subrectangular palisaded enclosure, were two buildings of far more massive construction than the rest (except for one other, also on the edge of the site). These

37 Excavated Romano-Celtic circular temple, Black Holmes, Thistleton, Leicestershire. Several buildings lay within a ditched *temenos*, one with a dedication by a Celt, Mocuxsoma, to a native deity, Veteris.

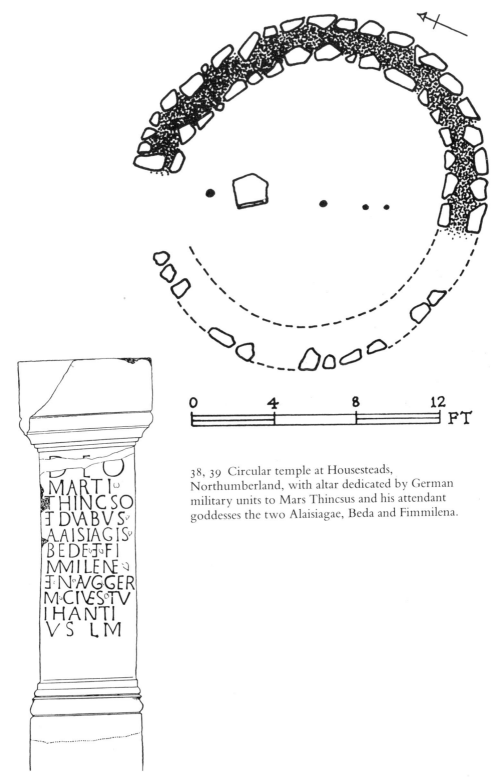

DEO
MARTI
THINCSO
ET DVABVS
A·AISIAGIS
BEDE·ET·FI
MMILENE
ET·N·AVGGER
M·CIVES·TV
IHANTI
VS·L·M

0 4 8 12
FT

38, 39 Circular temple at Housesteads,
Northumberland, with altar dedicated by German
military units to Mars Thincsus and his attendant
goddesses the two Alaisiagae, Beda and Fimmilena.

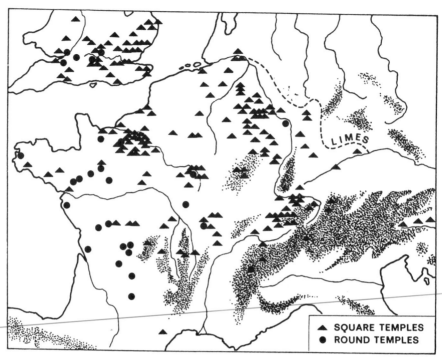

| ▲ | SQUARE TEMPLES |
| ● | ROUND TEMPLES |

40 Distribution map of double-square and circular Romano-Celtic temples.

have been interpreted as the houses of the chief, but the old problem rears its head – could not these just as well be temples within sanctuary enclosures? We really cannot say one way or the other, and the Goldberg neatly presents us with a crucial example of the predicament: Casterley in Wiltshire, described below, seems another instance.

SACRED ENCLOSURES

When we turn to open sanctuaries or sacral enclosures we encounter a complex and most intriguing series of sites. These must belong to the same early religious tradition that in Greece gave rise to the concept of the *temenos*, literally a 'cut' or share of land, here apportioned to the god, a 'consecrated and enclosed area surrounding the god's altar, which was the centre of worship and the only indispensable cult structure', and in the Roman world the same idea expressed in the original sense of the words *fanum* and *templum*. Whether the Celtic sanctuary-word *nemeton*, discussed below, included such precincts as well as natural woodland clearings is uncertain, but it could have done. Exceptionally we have structures circular in plan, as already noted at Frilford, and on a huge scale at the Goloring, an earthwork 625 feet in diameter near Koblenz, with a central post that may have stood 40 feet in height, and probably of the sixth century BC. The thermal springs of Les-Fontaines-Salées (Yonne) were surrounded in the first century AD with not only a double circular walled enclosure, but what appears to have been the bedding-trench for an oval of posts 30 by 50 feet, while circular or polygonal temples and enclosures take their place with the double-square type already mentioned in the Romano-Celtic series. But it should be stressed that there is no evidence for Celtic religious observances having been associated with Stonehenge, nor with any similar monument of the earlier second millennium BC. The extraordinary 'model Stonehenge' allegedly found by the Heidenmauer (Odilienberg) hill-fort in Alsace and illustrated by Kendrick seems to have been a reconstruction made more or less as a joke from a heap of stones believed by the excavator to have been a children's toy model of some sort of Celtic shrine: the fort itself has since been shown to belong to the fourth century AD.

There is a Gallo-Brittonic word *nemeton* which is used for a shrine or sanctuary in a sense that implies a sacred grove or clearing in a wood. The word is cognate with the Latin *nemus*, the primary sense of which (like that of *lucus*) is not so much a wood as a wood with a clearing in it, or the clearing itself within a grove. The most famous *nemus* was that of Diana at Aricia, where

> The priest who slew the slayer
> And shall himself be slain

held, uneasily, the title of *Rex Nemorensis*. Strabo records the name of the meeting-place of the council of the Galatians in Asia Minor as

41 Air photograph of part of the earthwork enclosures on the Hill of Tara, Co. Meath, Ireland, a traditional sacred centre and seat of temporal power.

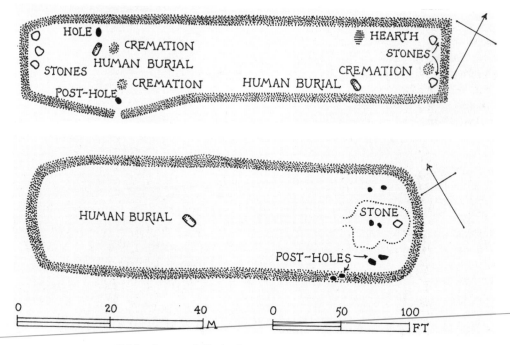

42, 43 Celtic elongated ditched sanctuary-enclosures at Aulnay-aux-Planches, Marne (probably tenth century BC) and Libenice, Czechoslovakia (third century BC).

Drunemeton, the sacred oak-grove, and Fortunatus writes in the sixth century AD of a place *Vernemet[on]* 'which in the Gaulish language means the great shrine' (using here the word *fanum*). Many *nemeton* place-names existed in the Celtic world, from *Medionemeton* in Southern Scotland, *Vernemeton* itself between Lincoln and Leicester and in Gaul, *Nemetodurum*, the modern Nanterre, to *Nemetobriga* in Spain. *Aquae Arnemetiae*, the modern Buxton, appears to show how the thermal springs there were associated with a sacred grove. In the eighth century 'forest sanctuaries which they call *nimidae*' are listed as heathen abominations, and in the eleventh, a Breton 'wood called Nemet' is recorded. The word and idea came through into Old Irish as *nemed*, a sanctuary, and *fidnemed*, a forest shrine or sacred grove.

41 The Irish site on the Hill of Tara in Co. Meath was a political and ceremonial centre traditionally deserted in the sixth century AD. Like other sites having 'royal' associations in early Ireland, such as Cruachan and Emain Macha, it is a complex of earthworks, one of which was found on excavation to be a mound covering a stone-chambered tomb dating from c. 2000 BC. The large circular earthwork known as The Rath of the Synods has also been partially excavated and has produced evidence of wooden structures and circular palisade enclosures presumed ritual, and dated by Roman imports between the first and third centuries AD. Very large quantities of animal bones might be taken to indicate sacrifices. There are other circular earthworks on the hill, and one rectangular enclosure referred to again below.

There are two remarkable sacral enclosures which share much the same elongated sub-rectangular plan although one is in the Marne and the other in Czechoslovakia: both however within the main central area of the early Celtic world. The French site at Aulnay-aux-Planches is the earlier, probably of the tenth century B C, and is enclosed by a ditch about 300 by 50 feet, with squared-off ends, lying north-east and south-west and with an entrance about a quarter of the way along the southern long side. This ditch may have held a palisade; inside were four burials including a possible sacrificed infant, and a pit containing a large ox skull, which might have been on a post set up in this hole, opposite the entrance.

42

The Czech site, at Libenice near Kolin in Bohemia, of the third century B C, is surrounded by a continuous ditch, oblong with slightly rounded ends, just under 300 feet long and 75 feet wide, with its axis north-west and south-east. At the south-east end had been some form of 'sanctuary' partly dug into the ground and perhaps, not certainly, roofed. It contained a stone stele and two close-set post-holes by which lay the charred remains of burnt-down uprights and two bronze neck-rings, reasonably interpreted as having adorned posts carved into human form. The pits making up the sunken sanctuary floor seem to have been dug one at a time, as if for repeated acts such as libations, and refilled over a period of time estimated at about 24 years. Animal and human bones

43, 44, 45

44, 45 Models of the Libenice sanctuary-site showing sunken area and standing posts.

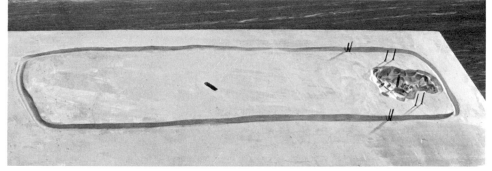

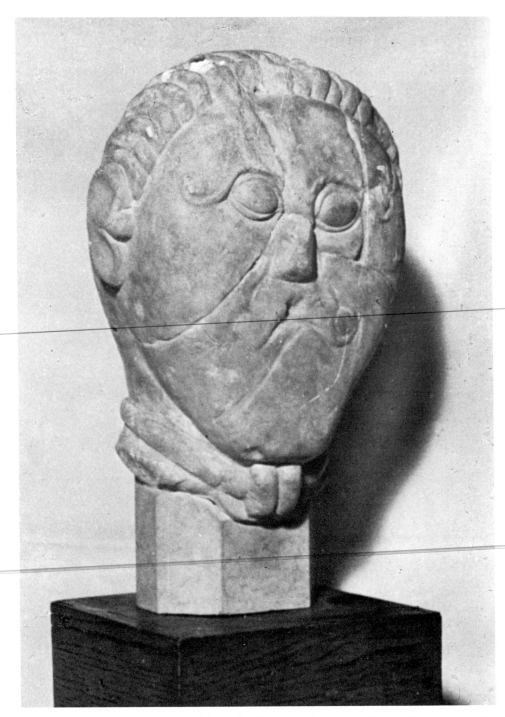

46 Stone sculpture of Celtic god or hero wearing a torc, found close by a double rectangular enclosure, at Mšecke Žehrovice, Czechoslovakia.

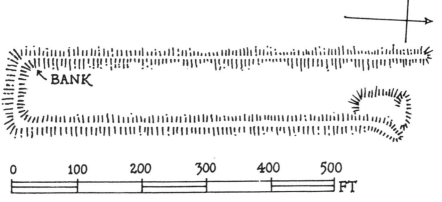

0   100   200   300   400   500   FT

47 Earthworks of the so-called 'Banqueting Hall' on the Hill of Tara, Ireland.

suggested sacrifices within the enclosure, which also contained the burial
of a woman, perhaps the priestess of the shrine. Another rectangular
sacred enclosure in Czechoslovakia is that at Mšecke Žehrovice, some   46
650 by 350 feet, from which came a notable life-size sculptured stone
head of a hero or god. The elongated plans of Aulnay and Libenice
prompt one to wonder whether the mysterious rectangular earthwork
on the Hill of Tara known as the Banqueting Hall, and measuring 750   47
by 90 feet, could not be something analogous.

   To return to the Marne, we have already seen that post-structures
were set inside small square ditched enclosures here, and in the Marne
these also are found enclosing graves, as elsewhere southwards to the
Yonne, eastwards to Czechoslovakia and northwards to Hertfordshire
and East Yorkshire in England. Other rectilinear or square enclosures
with contained structures or burials also occur, and the whole series
ranges in date from the fourth century BC to the eve of the Roman Conquest, thereafter to be reflected in the enclosed Roman cemeteries of
Gaul and Britain. The type has recently been shown to have an ancestry
going back at least as far as the early seventh century BC, as is shown by
the cremated burial in an urn of that date within a quadrilateral ditched
enclosure some 37 feet across, at Destelbergen in Belgium. A group of
cemeteries enclosed in square ditches and of late prehistoric or early
Roman date, concentrated south of Bonn, are probably representatives
of the same tradition.

   The lay-out of the angular ditched enclosures at Wallertheim in   48
Rheinhessen, belonging to this general series, recalls on a smaller scale
that of the Romano-British site by the side of the Roman road at its
intersection with Bokerly Dyke on the Wiltshire-Dorset border.   49, 50
Excavated by General Pitt-Rivers, the system of angular enclosure
ditches was found to contain an inhumation cemetery in a nearly square
ditched enclosure: if this area was a Romano-Celtic sanctuary site it
might account for the phenomenal number of coins found in the excavations immediately to the south, in a manner similar to the coin-scatter
outside the Romano-Celtic double-square temple at Woodeaton.

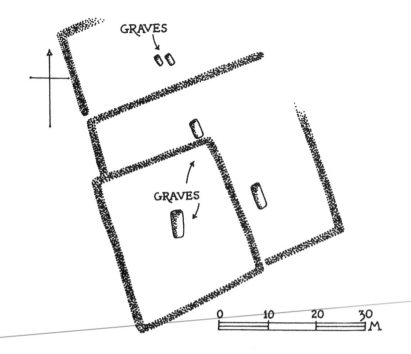

GRAVES

GRAVES

0 10 20 30
M

48, 49 Angular ditched enclosures and graves, late pre-Roman, at Wallertheim, Rheinhessen, and of the Roman period against the Roman road at Bokerly Dyke, Hampshire.

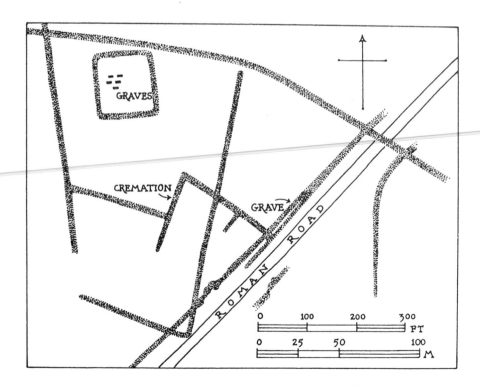

GRAVES

CREMATION

GRAVE

ROMAN ROAD

0 100 200 300
FT

0 25 50 100
M

50 Aerial view of Bokerly Dyke (native work of the Roman period) looking
east from the ditched enclosure area.

51 Aerial view of the early Iron Age hill-fort of Casterley, Wiltshire, with internal enclosures including a rectilinear area, perhaps for a shrine or temple.

51 Within the hill-fort of Casterley in Wiltshire excavations were carried out in a series of ditched enclosures centred on a rectilinear area about 200 feet square within a non-defensive ditch with external bank. Inside this again is an earlier ditched enclosure half the size (100 feet square): this was of late pre-Roman date, the larger enclosure being of the Roman period. The interior was not examined for timber structures, but evidence of rough paving was noted. The question of whether this is to be interpreted as a secular or a ritual focus of a temple-site cannot be dismissed out of hand. Such sites lead us to a remarkable group of sacral enclosures within the Celtic world, the rectilinear earthworks of the

52 German *Viereckschanze* type, in the main belonging to the last phase of native Celtic culture and continuing into Roman times, and interpreted as cult sites.

The main group of these has a compact distribution bounded on the south by the Alps from Lake Constance to Salzburg, and extending north to the River Main. There are outliers in Switzerland near Berne, and in eastern France, and a small secondary concentration between Chartres and the River Seine: field-work in France however would almost certainly alter this apparent pattern. Sites comparable with these (or with the other square enclosures just mentioned) may also exist

53 unrecognized as a class of Iron Age and Romano-British sacred sites in southern England. The Heath Row earthwork might be a claimant, and others seem likely, as for instance in Berkshire at Robin Hood's Arbour

54, 55 (Maidenhead), Ram's Hill (Uffington), Roden Downs (Compton) and

56 at Fox Furlong, Long Wittenham, where three rectangular enclosures each contained a well or shaft of a type to which we will shortly return.

52 Aerial view of ritual earthwork enclosure of *Viereckschanze* type, late pre-Roman Iron Age, at Buchendorf, near Munich, Bavaria.

53 Aerial view of ditched enclosure at Pavenham, Bedfordshire, unexcavated but perhaps related to continental enclosures of *Viereckschanze* type.

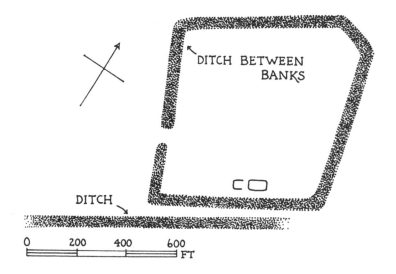

DITCH BETWEEN BANKS

DITCH

0 200 400 600 FT

At Bosence, St Erth (Cornwall) a square hill-top earthwork contained another such shaft. These possible examples appear to range in date from the final pre-Roman Belgic phase up to the fourth century A D. Our main knowledge of the German sites derives from the excavations still in progress at the Holzhausen *Viereckschanze* in Bavaria, which has produced some very remarkable evidence.

RITUAL SHAFTS

The earthwork at Holzhausen is nearly square, with a single entrance, enclosing an area nearly 300 feet across. This was found to have been preceded by two phases of timber palisade enclosures following the same perimeter, and within one corner a group of post-holes were interpreted as some form of rectangular shrine with a colonnade or ambulatory. Within and at the inner edge of the enclosing bank were three extraordinary ritual shafts, up to 8 feet in diameter and 120 feet deep. Similarly placed shafts are known in at least three other enclosures of the *Viereckschanze* type in Germany, and there must be many more unidentified. Two of the Long Wittenham enclosures, not hitherto considered in this context but apparently comparable, were 175 by 100 feet and 118 by 90 feet respectively, each containing a 'well' 8 feet deep, and a third irregularly angular ditch enclosed another shaft in an area 72 feet across. At Bosence, already mentioned, was a shaft 36 feet deep containing Roman votive deposits. With all these shafts go a very strange series of what have been called wells, funerary wells, or offering-pits, mostly Romano-Celtic and scattered over Gaul from the Rhineland to the Pyrenees and the Atlantic coast; in the German *Viereckschanze* area, and with an isolated example near the River Oder, and others in the Belgic area of south-eastern Britain, and associated with certain Romano-British temples.

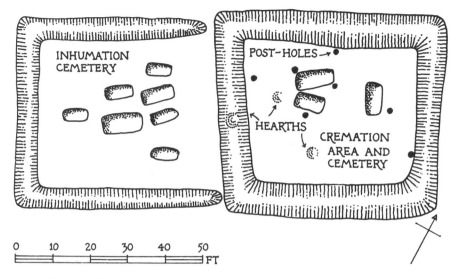

INHUMATION
CEMETERY

POST-HOLES →

HEARTHS

CREMATION
AREA AND
CEMETERY

0   10   20   30   40   50
FT

54, 55 Roman ditched enclosures, Roden Downs, Berkshire
(*opposite*), and details of inhumation cemetery and cremation area
(*above*).

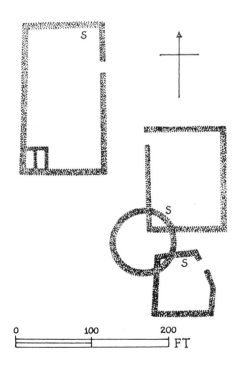

S

S

S

56 Ditched enclosures containing
ritual shafts (S), Fox Furlong, Long
Wittenham, Berkshire.

0   100   200
FT

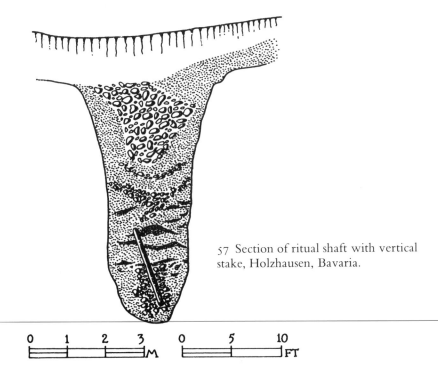

57 Section of ritual shaft with vertical stake, Holzhausen, Bavaria.

These examples are not contained within rectangular earthworks and their contents, which include deliberately placed deposits of objects such as pottery (often as whole vessels), animal and human bones, wooden figures in native or Roman idiom, and eccentricities such as a *58* 12-foot-high cypress stem (as at Le Bernard in Vendée), preclude one from regarding them as normal utilitarian wells: even if some were originally functional, they have taken on a markedly ritual character in their eventual history. At Holzhausen the shafts are regarded as emphatically not wells, and in one, some 25 feet deep, there was found a wooden stake set upright in the bottom, the filling around it containing material detectable by analysis as resulting from the breakdown of organic material such as flesh and blood. It seems probable that some of what have in the past been regarded as utilitarian deposits in many Roman wells (as rubbish, or as hoards hidden with intent to recover) might admit of an alternative explanation. What we seem to be encountering are the representatives of the cult concepts which found expression in the Greek *bothros* and the Latin *mundus*, ritual shafts communicating with other-world deities, and in the *favissa*, the pit in which objects rendered holy by sacral use, and the bones or ashes of sacrifices, were buried in the consecrated area. Evidence from barbarian Europe shows us that such shafts have an ancestry going back to the middle of the second millennium BC. It has been suggested that a well-known scene on the Gun-*61* destrup cauldron, of the first century BC, shows not a ritual drowning or immersion in a vessel as previously suggested, but the deposition

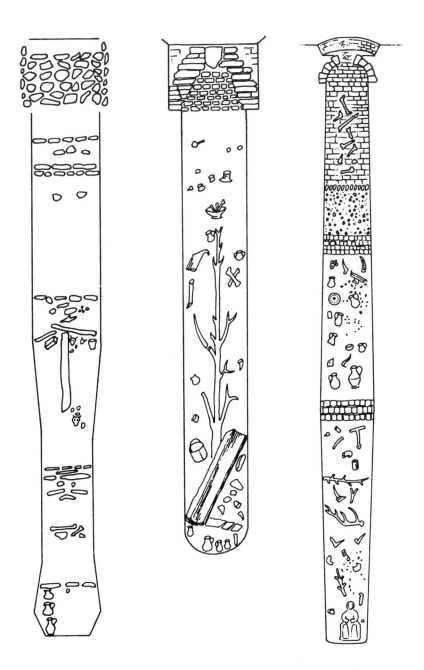

58 Sections of ritual shafts in the Vendée, showing objects deposited in the filling. The shaft on the right is 12.5 m deep.

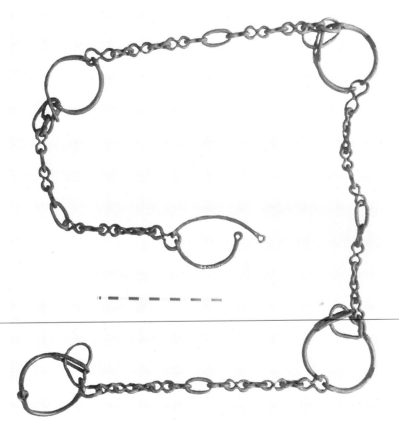

59 Iron chain for a slave-gang, from the early Iron Age votive deposit at Llyn Cerrig Bach, Anglesey.

of the victim in a sacred shaft, with an uprooted tree carried by a file of foot-soldiers on their spear-points, comparable to the cypress in the shaft in Vendée mentioned above.

VOTIVE DEPOSITS

These ritual shafts, some of which may also have functioned at one time as wells, link the Celtic cult of the underworld with that of springs and water. Here we have a deep-rooted set of beliefs still surviving vigorously into modern Celtic folk-lore and attested in antiquity by numerous finds reasonably explicable as votive in character, and deposited in pools, springs, or natural wells. Examples of such finds in the Celtic world are numerous, and even if some (like the hoards in Roman wells) may alternatively be explained as merely utilitarian in intention, others remain stubbornly votive in character. The second or third century BC deposit of two thousand objects, mostly brooches and bracelets in a cauldron, at the Giants' Springs at Duchcov in Czechoslovakia seems a case in point, as does the site of La Tène itself on Lake Neuchâtel, or Llyn Cerrig

59, 60

60 Decorative bronze mounting, from the early Iron Age votive deposit at Llyn Cerrig Bach, Anglesey.

Bach in Anglesey, or the cauldron-finds in lakes like some in southern Scotland, or of course Gundestrup. The classical writers bear witness to Gaulish treasures, exposed but inviolate in native sanctuaries, and one, the Treasure of Toulouse, was pillaged by the Consul Caepio in 106 B C – Posidonius describes it as in sacred precincts and pools and its weight was estimated as 100,000 lb. of gold and 110,000 lb. of silver. Gregory of Tours in the sixth century A D describes a Gallo-Roman lakeside festival in the Cevennes, with animal sacrifices and votive offerings thrown into the water: annual meetings continued here until 1868!

CAULDRONS

Cauldrons themselves, their manufacture made possible by the techno-logical expertise of Celtic metal-smiths, could be sacred vessels, and beyond the Celtic world the Cimbri sent to Augustus 'the most sacred cauldron in their country' as a diplomatic gift. Strabo, recording this, goes on to describe the sacrifice of prisoners of war by cutting their throats over such a vessel, and in the Celtic world the well-known pas-

61 Detail of repoussé silver plate from the ceremonial cauldron found as a votive deposit at Gundestrup, Himmerland, Denmark, showing the ceremonial drowning of a victim in a tub.

62 Stone carving of
a head with ritual
'leaf-crown',
fifth-fourth century
BC, from Heidelberg,
Germany.

sage in the Berne scholia on Lucan's lines about Gaulish deities describes
sacrifices to Teutates – 'a man is put head-first into a full tub, so that he is
suffocated'. We have seen that there may be a representation of this very
rite on the Gundestrup cauldron. Wells with votive offerings are fre-   61
quent in Romano-Celtic contexts, as at Coventina's Well on Hadrian's
Wall, with human skulls among the votive gifts, and the severed head
continues its association with wells and springs in modern Celtic belief.

IMAGES

We have already touched on representational sculpture of human beings,
or of the head alone: probably as a result of ultimate Greek or Etruscan
influence it was known in the Celtic world from the sixth century BC
onwards. Stone sculpture has naturally the best chance of survival, as the   62
Hirschlanden, Holzehrlingen or Pfalzfeld pieces show, the Mšecke   46
Žehrovice head, the Euffigneix (Marne) man-boar sculpture, or the
earlier carved stone heads and non-representational omphaloid stones
such as Turoe or Castle Strange in Ireland, all in a native artistic idiom.   68
In bronze there are pieces such as the Bouray (Seine-et-Oise) squatting
male figure in sections of cast and beaten metal, or the Tarbes head and
many other related works of pre-Roman date.

In exceptional circumstances wooden figures have survived, as perhaps
69 that from the Lake of Geneva, or a series of undated figures from the
British Isles. In Gaul, there are those from a shaft at Montbouy near
Orléans, others from Essarois (Côte-d'Or), and the astonishing collection of nearly 200 wooden sculptures from what must have been a Celtic
sanctuary at the source of the River Seine, including human and animal
63–7   representations as well as those of internal organs, these last presumably
votive or associated with divination in a manner recalling Etruscan
practices. Pre-Roman Celtic religious sculpture in wood may have been
far more abundant than we have thought in the past. Lucan, in a highly
wrought passage of nevertheless impressive poetry, describing a Celtic
forest-sanctuary near Massalia violated and destroyed by Caesar,
explicitly refers to such sculptures:

> And there were many
> dark springs running there, and grim-faced figures of gods uncouthly
> hewn by the axe from the untrimmed tree-trunk, rotted to whiteness.

Behind the rhetoric, the basic picture in Lucan is convincing – the
nemeton, or holy place in the dark frightening wood, the sacred springs
and pools, and the wooden figures carved in the artistic idiom of the
Celts, so primitive and alien to the classical schema of the accurate
delineation of the human form that they well deserved the phrase *arte
carent*. Such figures may well have been the 'many images' seen by
Caesar or his informants: so too it looks as though Gildas, writing of
Britain in the sixth century AD, was describing later Celtic sculptures,
perhaps also in wood, with their grotesque, stiff and savage features,
which he saw and deplored all around him.

63 Part of a deposit of over
5,000 wood figures and other
carvings round the spring of
Les Roches, Chamalières
(Auvergne), early Gallo-
Roman: a recent discovery even
more dramatic than that at the
source of the Seine.

64 Wooden votive head from the source of the Seine.
65 Wooden figure showing internal organs from
Chamalières. 66 Wooden votive figure from the
source of the Seine. 67 Wooden post carved with
three heads from the source of the Seine.

68 Stone carved with La Tène ornament, end of first century BC, at Turoe, Co. Galway, Ireland.

69 Head of wooden phallic figure
from Shercock or Ralaghan, Co.
Cavan, Ireland.

70 Limestone head, Romano-Celtic sculpture of first century AD (or perhaps medieval), from Gloucester.

71 Stone head, Romano-Celtic, from near the Roman road at Appleby, Cumbria.

72 Head from Romano-Celtic stone statue from a shrine dedicated to Antenociticus at Benwell, Northumberland.

We saw in the first chapter some of the difficulties inherent in the interpretation of the large number of Gaulish and (to a less extent) British god-names known from inscriptions. An interesting point is that on the whole the British dedications form a group not duplicated on the Continent, demonstrating not only the insular particularity of the British Celtic tradition (visible also in material culture) but also the bewildering number of rustic godlings with only a very local reputation and name. It has been possible to define the areas of local cults in Gaul on a rather larger scale however: examples are the three-headed god, mainly in the Marne and Côte-d'Or; the wheel-bearing deity, extending to the Massif Central and the lower Rhône, or the god with a hammer, popular in the Midi, up the Rhône, and on to the Seine and the Rhineland. These do not conform to the known political boundaries of the Celtic tribes, but a 'divine couple' have been assigned to the Aedui. Other iconographic types, such as the horned god, or the two-faced 'Janus' type, have a widely scattered distribution throughout the Gaulish area. What seems mainly brought out by iconographic and epigraphic studies is the enormous diversity and parochiality that the aspects of the Celtic deities could assume, and the impossibility of trying to reduce to a system a scheme where no system need have existed, and where inconsistencies were irrelevant, or of making equations with an alien and less ambivalent pantheon, as the Roman writers tried.

With the adoption of the provincial Roman artistic tradition, stone
sculpture was used in Celtic religious and funerary contexts on an ex-
tensive scale, and here we have iconography supported by epigraphy,
when the god–name or attribute is given in an accompanying inscription.
Side-by-side with this adoption of the Mediterranean artistic schema the
native idiom did however continue, especially in the carving of severed
heads in stone, as in North Britain or in Ireland, but the *Antenociticus*
head from Benwell on Hadrian's Wall is broken from a statue and not a
complete piece in itself.

70, 71

72

FUNERARY RITUAL

There remains one aspect of the archaeology of Celtic religion important in our present enquiry, the inferences we can draw from burials.
Here the outstanding characteristics, in common with a long series from
barbarian Europe, are on the one hand the reflection of a socially stratified society in the elaborate and costly burials furnished with the equipment of an heroic or an aristocratic class, and on the other the inherent
implication of a very literal view of an after–life in the contents of these
graves. Royal tombs, chieftains' graves and the like appear in the
archaeological record as the recurrent expression of societies of broadly
speaking 'heroic' type, whether in the mid second millennium B C in the
Wessex or Central European bronze-using cultures, or those contemporary but more highly civilized in Shang Dynasty China, or later
among the Celts or Scythians. From the seventh century B C to the point
of Romanization such tombs occur in a Celtic context, the men's graves
often provided with a four-wheeled or two-wheeled vehicle as well as
martial equipment, with the inescapable implication that an other-
world is thought of as one where earthly status is recognized and pro-
longed to eternity. In a group of graves in immediately pre-Roman
Belgic Britain – Welwyn, Stanfordbury, Mount Bures and others –
there is provision not only for the chieftain's feast beyond the tomb, but
for a guest, with twin double fire-dogs and wine in amphorae totalling
some seven dozen bottles apiece in modern terms.

73

We will return to the significance of this in the next chapter when we
come to consider the concepts of immortality attributed to the Celts by
the classical writers, but we may here note how archaeology is corroborated by texts in this respect. The customs just noted, with burial by
inhumation or by cremation, are explicitly specified in the surviving
text of a Romano-Celtic testamentary statement from the tribal area of
the Lingones in Gaul (around the upper Marne), where the deceased
orders to be burnt with him his river boat, and his hunting and wild-
fowling tackle, and directs his funerary monument to be built in detailed
terms reminiscent of Browning's Bishop ordering his tomb in St
Praxed's. The classical writers had noted this literal concept of personal
immortality with surprise. 'Funerals,' wrote Caesar, 'considering the
Gaulish standard of living, are splendid and costly, everything, even
including animals, which the departed is supposed to have cared for

73 Iron bull-headed stand, perhaps for holding wine-amphorae, from a Belgic grave with provision for feasting, Welwyn, Hertfordshire.

when alive, is consigned to the flames.' Slaves and retainers, he goes on, were sacrificed until shortly before the time of his campaigns. Pomponius Mela in the first century AD makes the same point about the Gauls – 'they burn or bury with the dead the things they were accustomed to in life.' The feeling permeates the Gallo-Roman sculptured tombs with banquet scenes 'in which individuals copied from life sit round a table, reflecting the Gaulish mood for anecdote' and comes out in the naive interior sculpture of the Simpelveld sarcophagus from Batavia, referred to again in the next chapter, where we shall see how the classical world came to construct its picture of the Celtic beliefs in immortality.

SUMMARY: THE DRUIDS' WORLD AND ITS ORIGINS

Describing the Irish world as seen in the earliest vernacular literature, Binchy summarized it as 'tribal, rural, hierarchical, and familiar', and this would equally apply to the pre-Roman Celtic world at large, even if shortly before the Conquest Gaul was moving into something a little nearer to a rustic approximation of Mediterranean modes in some superficial respects. In its essentials it was a barbarian world of a type from which the peoples of the classical world had been increasingly diverging over many centuries in their developing civilizations, even though they had once shared the same background. It was alien in language and thought, belief and custom, manners and conventions, social structure and scale of values. It must have taken much the same place in the emotions and imaginations of Greeks and Romans as the American Indians or the Irish to the Elizabethans, or as did the world of the Scottish Highlanders, or of the Polynesians of Tahiti, in those of English citizens of the eighteenth century.

Such barbaric culture-patterns had long existed in Europe north of the Alps, and indeed go back in part to an ancestry shared by the Greeks and Romans themselves, and other speakers of the Indo-European languages. We need not claim exclusive rights within this language group for the social system of elective ruler, council of elders or nobles, and assembly of freemen, which appears to have existed in ancient Sumer and need not be Indo-European in its Hittite manifestation, though it could be. The tripartite division of classes has been called in question as a valid concept, and of course even if its existence is admitted need not be only Indo-European, but it is in this linguistic setting that many scholars have identified such a phenomenon, with *brahmans*, *flamines* and *druides*, *equites* and *kshatriyas*, *plebes* and *vaishyas*, across Eurasia from Celtic Ireland, past early Rome, and to Sanskrit-speaking India. The Celtic tradition in Ireland conserved untouched archaisms in language, ideas and even prosody which have their counterparts in Sanskrit or Hittite, and we must be seeing fragments of a common heritage that goes back to the second millennium BC.

The archaeological evidence for Celtic religious practices immediately confronts us, as we have seen, with comparisons of *temenos*, *bothros* and *mundus* in the classical world, and in pre-historic Europe this archaism is again perceptible, with the Goloring or Frilford echoing the British Henge Monuments of the later third or early second millennium B C, as Aulnay and Libenice recall the contemporary *cursus* structures. But here we should repeat that there is no archaeological evidence for associating Early Iron Age, let alone Druid, ritual performances with Stonehenge or any other circle of earlier date. The ritual shafts however have their best parallels in sites such as Wilsford (Wilts.) and Swanwick (Hants.) pits, both datable to the second half of the second millennium B C, and at Swanwick with an upright post and blood remains as at Holzhausen.

It is against such a cultural background as that sketched in this chapter that we must set Celtic religion, and with it the bards, the seers, and the Druids. It would be an error in method to consider the comments of the classical writers in isolation from this credible and consistent anthropological picture of the society which they encountered, and about which they wrote. The Greeks and Romans knew much about the Celts we shall never know, and one wishes more had been transmitted to us, but on the other hand we also know things about the Celts, and indeed about the classical world, not known to Posidonius or to Caesar, let alone to Diviciacus.

74 The Scythian world: electrum vase (full size) made in a Greek Black Sea colony (probably Panticapaeum) for the local market and showing scenes of Scythian life. From a princely tumulus-grave at Kul Oba, fourth century BC now in the Hermitage, Leningrad (electrotype copy in the Victoria & Albert Museum, London).

Chapter Three

THE DRUIDS IN THE
CLASSICAL AND
VERNACULAR TEXTS

THE GREEK AND LATIN TEXTS

We have already briefly indicated, in the first chapter, some of the
difficulties inherent in our understanding of the documentary sources
referring to the Druids, especially in the group of Greek and Latin texts.
Turning now to these in greater detail, the first factor to be borne in
mind is that we are dealing with a particular instance of a general situation, the emotional and intellectual impact made upon a civilized people
by contact with others in a more barbarous state of culture. The Greeks
had long been aware that on the northern edges of their known world
there were peoples not only of alien culture, such as were Chaldeans or
Persians or Egyptians, but at a lower stage of technological achievement
and of social and political organization. A broad grouping visualized
two main barbarian peoples in the European land-mass, Scythians in the
north-east and Celts in the north-west, with Iberians in the far western
peninsula and a vague penumbra of remote tribes, including those
named Hyperboreans, beyond Scythian or Celtic territory. Actual
contacts began to replace rumour with the establishment of the Black
Sea colonies from the seventh century BC onwards, and in the west the
foundation of Massalia about 600 BC gave contacts with the Celtic
world.

74

PRIMITIVISM

In the next chapter we shall see how the Greek experience can be
paralleled by the European encounter with primitive peoples from the
first discovery of the Americas to that of the South Sea Islands in the
second half of the eighteenth century. Historians of ideas have studied
these and other comparable situations, from antiquity to modern times,
in terms of the views held by the civilized protagonists of such con-
frontations about the less advanced peoples – in other words, the concept of 'primitivism'. If we begin by looking at the classical sources for
the Druids in such terms we immediately find we can distinguish here
two main contrasted viewpoints about the barbarians which run in fact

91

throughout all Western thought on the subject. Mrs Chadwick in her recent discussion of these sources made a division of them into two groups, distinguished not only by contrasted moods of feeling about the Celts, but by their chronological contexts. The earlier group she names from the main classical writer on the Celts, Posidonius, a Syrian Greek from Apamaea (c. 135–c. 50 BC): this 'Posidonian' tradition is often unfavourable to the Celts and does not minimize their barbarous habits. The second, or 'Alexandrian' group is centred on later writers in the scholastic tradition of Alexandria, and presents a more sympathetic and idealized version. What is so interesting is that in making this division, she was not concerned with the history of ideas as such, yet nevertheless draws, in respect of these sources on the Druids, the precise distinction made between what has been called 'hard' and 'soft' primitivism by historians of ideas such as Lovejoy and Boas. In hard primitivism, usually as a result of first-hand contact with the more barbarous culture, a realistic and often unflattering view is taken, and the descriptions will be empirical and factual; in soft primitivism distance in time or space lends enchantment to the view, and desirable qualities are not only sought for, but discovered and idealized. The sequence frequently moves from soft to hard, progressing from vague travellers' tales and rumours to actual colonization and exploration of barbarian territory; the classical world's reactions to the Black Sea peoples are curious, appearing to move, despite first-hand knowledge from the first, from the noble Scythians of earlier Greek tradition to Ovid's pungent comments as an exile among the Getae. But with the Celts, and so with the Druids, first-hand experience by such as Posidonius, Caesar or Tacitus had priority over the indirect knowledge of later writers seeking confirmation of philosophical speculations.

It would be pedantic to insist on a strict adherence to pattern in either tradition, and indeed the individual largely responsible for the earlier information on the Druids, Posidonius, can only be considered a hard primitivist with a rather soft centre. In part an empirical observer, his position as an exponent of Stoic philosophy favoured an idealization of primitive peoples. His viewpoint was recognized and acknowledged in antiquity: one of those who used his work, Athenaeus (who was, to coin a word, a gastrologue, writing on wining and dining in about AD 200), refers to his source as 'the Stoic philosopher Posidonius, describing many customs and many peoples in his *Histories*, which work he composed in accordance with his philosophical convictions.' These, as a modern scholar has written, included a belief that political virtue 'consists in turning humanity back to its state of prehistoric innocence' and 'his study of primitive cultures led him to establish the principle that the present condition of semi-civilized peoples reflects the original state of culture among those now civilized.' Such views, in a prevailing somewhat pessimistic climate of thought, led to a longing to find happier times or happier peoples in the past or beyond the fringe of civilization, and another Stoic philosopher, the Roman Seneca, writing in the early first century AD, gives us not only a summary of the Posidonian position with regard to primitive peoples but the key phrase for the basic concept behind soft primitivism. 'In that age we call golden,' he wrote, 'Posidonius holds that rulership was confided to the wise.'

We glanced at the concept of The Golden Age in chapter I, and saw how it came to be thought of as remote in either time or space: this is chronological or cultural primitivism. The expression of the idea of a past Golden Age goes back to Hesiod and beyond, where the golden quality may be that of the people, not of their metal technology as in the Ages of Bronze and Iron; in Homer the concepts are partly of an afterworld paradise on 'the Elysian plain and the world's end', and partly of contemporary noble, golden-hearted barbarians living on or beyond the northern edges of the known world:

'the proud Hippomulgoi,
drinkers of milk, and the Abioi, most righteous of all men'.

Herodotus in the fifth century BC adds the Argippaei, north of the Scythians; virtuous, vegetarian peace-makers who have no warfare nor weapons. A century later, Ephorus makes the Scythians themselves play an idealized role: they 'feed on mare's milk and excel all men in justice'. They preserved this reputation up to Strabo's time at the end of the first century BC – 'we regard the Scythians', he writes, 'as the most just of men and the least prone to mischief, as also far more frugal and independent of others than we are.' In many minds there has been firmly set 'the recurrent notion of an original life of simplicity and virtue, from which we ourselves have lamentably declined, though it may still survive among distant and little-known peoples'.

THE HYPERBOREANS

The most distinguished of all claimants for the title of Noble Savages in antiquity however were the Hyperboreans, worshippers of Apollo and dwelling beyond the North Wind. They are of importance to us here not only for their place as idealized barbarians in general, but because they did in fact become inextricably bound up in the beliefs built up around Celts, Druids and followers of Pythagoras. Theirs is a complex story, seemingly part mythological invention, part genuine tradition, and part wishful thinking, but we must at least consider its outlines.

Aristeas of Proconnesus in the seventh century BC seems to have made a genuine journey, or journeys, into Scythian territory and beyond, reaching at least the fringes of peoples who knew something of Central Asia. The Hyperboreans as a mythical race of peaceful, happy, virtuous and vegetarian people, beloved by Apollo and living in a northern Never-Never Land, already existed in legend, and, as a mystical and ecstatic votary of Apollo, Aristeas went to find them. There now arises a fascinating situation: he seems to have heard tales of people whose qualities approximated to the myth, and these, more than one scholar has suggested, might be no other than the civilized Chinese, then under the Eastern Chou dynasty. His informants would have been Central

Asian nomads: 'to semi-savages living hard and dangerously the ordered society of China might well appear a model of peace, justice and luxury; and to men whose staple food was meat the agricultural Chinese, whose staple food was cereal, could well appear as vegetarians.' But whether we accept this most intriguing identification or not, from Aristeas onwards the Hyperboreans were being literally put on the map as a real people.

The map in question would have presented itself in general terms as a great semi-circular area of territory north of the Black Sea and the Mediterranean, bounded by the River Oceanus and containing two main tribal groups, Scyths to the east and Celts to the west, with more vaguely apprehended peoples, including the Hyperboreans, beyond these but still within the limits of Ocean. It was generally agreed that their territory lay beyond the Rhipaean Mountains, but these themselves were of uncertain geographical location. Herodotus, who regarded the Hyperboreans as a myth and joked about their name, nevertheless puts their country beyond that of the Scythians, as did others of his time and later, together with the mountains. Now several early Greek writers, such as Pindar and Aeschylus, thought the River Danube also rose in these same heights, and indeed Aeschylus wrote of it as flowing 'from the Hyperboreans and the Rhipaean Mountains'.

As Herodotus makes the Danube rise in Celtic territory, quite correctly, we can see the geographical conflation that could ensue, and how Posidonius himself could equate the Rhipaean Mountains with the Alps and place the Hyperboreans beyond these, for before him a writer in the late fourth century BC could think that Rome had been sacked in c. 390 by Hyperboreans and not by Celts, and Hecateus of Abdera had located them, and their mysterious and magnificent temple of Apollo, in the British Isles.

Once Hyperboreans and Celts had become merged in a northern twilight, it was of course possible for the mythical or legendary characteristics of the former to be attributed to the latter. Their country gets confused with the Elysian plains and the realm of Rhadamanthus in Homer – 'no snow is there nor yet any great storm nor any rain' is the phrase in the Odyssey, and Pliny (in Philemon Holland's enchanting 1601 translation) says of the Hyperboreans:

> their countrie is open upon the sun, of a blissful and pleasant temperature, void of all noisome wind and hurtful aires. Their habitations be in woods and groves, where they worship the gods both of themselves, and in companies and congregations: no discord know they, no sicknesse are they acquainted with.

It was left for Tennyson, in *The Passing of Arthur*, to write of:

> the island-valley of Avilion
> Where falls not hail, or rain, or any snow,
> Nor ever wind blows loudly

and so to combine the Homeric and the Hyperborean Shangri-la in his Victorian Celtic Britain.

Behind both the Posidonian and the Alexandrian traditions about the Druids there was then the myth of the Noble Savage as a potential source of confusion. The classical world, on its first contact with the Celts, was already prepared to find certain expected elements in a primitive culture such as theirs. The society would of course be less complex and sophisticated than that of the civilized Mediterranean, but this simplicity would be a virtue, preserving ancient and uncorrupted traditions of rugged integrity lost in the debasing and enervating complications of city life. In those days of primal innocence men walked close to the gods and knew intuitively the secrets of nature now only to be apprehended dimly and with difficulty by the philosophers, and in nature's simple plan the wise men were the acknowledged rulers, guiding secular princes in the ways of justice, equity and learning. In the late first century A D Clement of Alexandria, of the idealizing school, even went so far as to claim that Pythagorean and other Greek philosophy was acquired from the Gauls and other barbarians.

It is worth while pausing for a moment here to consider an epithet, taken almost certainly from Posidonius by Strabo, as we shall see, and applied to the Druids: they are considered to be 'the most just' or 'the most righteous' (*dikaiotatoi*) of men. On first sight an interesting tribute to the probity of Celtic law-givers, the phrase loses some of its force when we realize that it is a stock literary attribute in Greek, going back as we saw to Homer, who applies it to the Abioi. It is taken up by Herodotus in respect of the Getae, and by Ephorus of the Scythians; and it is used by Strabo himself not only of the Druids, but of Scyths and Mysians as well as the obvious law-givers Moses and Rhadamanthus – the latter, it will be remembered, ruling those Elysian plains that seemed so similar to the land of the Hyperboreans. 'Most just men' were to be expected in primitive societies and so were Golden Ages, where indeed (as we saw) Seneca said that Posidonius thought the wise men were the rulers. We shall also see later on how this view may have coloured another attribute of the Druids, their power to intervene in war.

Legend recorded not only barbarian philosophers in general, but some individuals as well. Abaris the Hyperborean disputed in Greek with Pythagoras himself: Professor Dodds has persuasively argued that if he existed at all, he might well have been a Central Asian shaman. Anacharsis was an expatriate Scythian philosopher, and we move insensibly towards those not necessarily philosophers, but high-minded nobles, such as the Scythian chieftain who addressed Alexander in an elevating speech. We must look later at these set speeches by barbarian chiefs, part of the stock-in-trade of ancient historians and familiar to us in British legend as uttered by Boudica and Calgacus, for such literary conventions must lie behind the picture given to us by Caesar and Cicero of Diviciacus, the Gaulish chieftain who also appears to have been a Druid.

The world of the Celtic Druids will then have been approached with a number of presuppositions already in the minds of even the most unprejudiced men of letters who were to write about it in antiquity. To the philosophers, especially to those in the Stoic tradition, the idea of sages as rulers among remote primitive peoples would naturally make an irresistible appeal, much as some scientists today might like to think of an Utopia in which their counterparts, rather than politicians, were the governors. And there is one final point to make in general about the reports the classical writers give of the learning and knowledge of the Druids. In any such descriptions they could not escape the use of a technical vocabulary which was the result of centuries of profound and subtle thinking, and which had therefore acquired overtones of intellectual complexity and sophistication, but which had to be used in recording the simplest beliefs, superstitions, traditional lore and institutions of the barbarian peoples beyond the Alps. They could not escape from writing of *philosophoi* and *theologoi*, philosophers and theologians; who studied *physiologia* and *ethike philosophia*, natural and moral philosophy; investigated *quaestiones occultarum rerum alterumque*, problems of things secret and sublime; and were *magistri sapientiae*, professors of wisdom. It would surely be a mistake to think that such phrases when applied to the Druids should necessarily be interpreted in the same sense as in a Socratic dialogue or a passage of Seneca or Cicero.

THE POSIDONIAN TRADITION

With these preliminaries we can now turn to the two groups of classical texts and their relationships, and then, after a shorter glance at the Irish sources, go on to examine one by one the main features they attribute to the Druids. The Posidonian group of sources, as we saw, are in the main closely linked to the work of the Stoic philosopher himself, and have been brilliantly analysed by Professor Tierney. The situation is briefly as follows. The *Histories* of Posidonius, written at the end of the second century B C, exist today only in second-hand quotations, acknowledged or identifiable, in other writers, but originally consisted of 52 books beginning where Polybius left off in the mid second century and dealing not only with Graeco-Roman history but with the foreign peoples encountered by the classical world at this time. The section dealing with the Celts was in Book 23, and formed an ethnographical introduction to an account of the Roman conquest and occupation of southern Gaul ending in 121 B C with the creation of the *Provincia Romana*. Posidonius travelled in Gaul himself, and used Massaliot sources. He was an outstanding scholar in the long-established Greek tradition of historical, geographical and ethnographic research going back to Herodotus, searching 'for the true origins by studying the common qualities and family likenesses of nations', as Strabo put it, and, as we saw, likely to interpret his data in terms of Stoic philosophy.

Four main writers seem to have borrowed, quoted from, or adapted Posidonius, three explicitly and one without acknowledgement. Strabo (c. 63 B C to A D 21) had known Posidonius personally; Diodorus Siculus (writing c. 60–30 B C) was also a contemporary; Athenaeus (flourishing around A D 200) acknowledged his source. Julius Caesar, however, writing his account of the Gaulish campaigns in 52–51 B C, seems also to have based his account of Gaulish ethnography (including the Druids) on Posidonius, though with non-Posidonian additions, the authenticity and reliability of which have been the subject of much discussion. Strabo and Diodorus were writing geography and history very much in the Posidonian manner; Athenaeus was a gourmet compiling an erudite and entertaining anthology; Caesar was an astute politician and military commander writing self-justificatory despatches after the event. Of the four, Athenaeus alone does not mention Druids, who were perhaps irrelevant to him, as not having been recorded to have given dinner-parties.

The viewpoint presented by the four writers is factual and the general picture of Celtic manners and customs which emerges from their Posidonian quotations or paraphrases is consistent with that contained in other writers such as Polybius writing before Posidonius, or Pomponius Mela, Lucan or Tacitus rather later. It is also consonant with that depicted in the Irish hero-tales discussed below and with the inferences to be made from archaeological evidence. There is a certain amount of soft primitivism in presenting the knowledge, status and authority of the Druids, and Caesar here lays emphasis on their political power in a manner not found in any other source. His divergencies from the Posidonian canon will be noted below under specific topics: some of his additional material may well derive from genuine first-hand information, but as Tierney has said, 'Caesar had no interest in Gallic ethnography as such', and the ethnographical passages in Book VI of the *Gallic Wars* are there because literary convention ruled that historical works should contain such a section. The original Celtic ethnography of Posidonius was after all in the same relationship to an historical treatise. The whole of the *Gallic Wars* is a very carefully constructed document. 'The brilliant brevity of Caesar has at times encouraged the view that his style is the straight, plain writing of a simple soldier,' Michael Grant writes, but goes on, 'the truth is rather that Caesar's apparent simplicity, and lack of rhetoric, were deliberate artifices based on mastery of the most elaborate rhetorical theory.' His general Hirtius (who wrote the concluding Book VIII of the work) seems to have been well aware of this. 'Caesar not only wrote with supreme fluency and elegance,' he said, 'he also knew superlatively well how to describe his plans and policies.'

But to return to the Posidonian account of the Druids, if it has an element of soft primitivism in it, this is counterbalanced by a frank description of attendant barbarities such as human sacrifice. There has been, as we shall see, a recent attempt to exculpate the Druids from participation in such barbarous practices, but this seems a desperate effort to maintain soft primitivism in a very hard situation. Perhaps, as Zeno in the third century B C had actually argued that cannibalism might not be immoral 'in certain circumstances' among primitive peoples, some Stoics might have found it acceptable, but Posidonius reports it as another barbarity, on a par with the Celtic chieftains' head-hunting.

After these three primary sources, there follows a group of writers of less importance for their general comments on Celtic manners and customs but important to us because they do talk about the Druids. Of these, Ammianus Marcellinus, a historian of the fourth century AD, used earlier sources, including Timagenes, who wrote in the first century BC, and who is also quoted on the Druids by Diodorus. Lucan, in the first century AD, was a poet describing Caesar's military successes, and stresses, for his own rhetorical purposes, the barbaric strangeness of Celtic religion, as do the *scholia* or commentaries added to a Lucan manuscript at Berne between the fourth and ninth centuries. Pomponius Mela, a geographer writing about the same time, again gives an account in a Posidonian mood of hard primitivism. The elder Pliny wrote a discursive and fascinating work on natural history in the same century, in which mention of Druid magic, simples and folk-medicine occurs in his entries on oak trees, mistletoe, snakes' eggs and so on. Finally Tacitus in his *Annals* gives us, in a mood of very hard primitivism indeed, our only glimpse of British Druids, like howling Dervishes, ritually cursing the Roman troops by the Menai Straits. But it is interesting to remember that his *Germania* has many elements of soft primitivism, as by implication it compares the hardiness of the barbarians with the effete society of contemporary Rome.

THE ALEXANDRIAN TRADITION

This group of sources does not involve such complications of derivation and relationship as the central core of the Posidonian texts, though borrowings clearly exist. As Mrs Chadwick points out, the Alexandrian sources are in the main 'Greek texts written by scholars educated in the School of Alexandria from at least as early as the first century AD onwards'. The consistent viewpoint is that of soft primitivism, or, as she puts it, the mood 'however erroneous at times in the interpretation of the traditions, is in tone respectful towards the druids' and 'discusses their philosophy on the level of other systems beyond the limits of the Ionian and the Greek world.' The elements of soft primitivism present (as we saw) in the Posidonian tradition are taken up and enlarged upon, and especially the alleged connections with the doctrines of Pythagoras, while equations are made between Druids, Egyptian priests, Persian *magi* and Indian brahmins. It is all second-hand library work, with no new empirical observations from first-hand informants or from fieldwork among the Celtic peoples. Dio Chrysostom and Hippolytus, Diogenes Laertius and Polyhistor lead on to the early Church fathers, Clement, Cyril and Origen, up to the third century AD, in works of synthesis and collation. Occasionally a more valuable piece of information is preserved, as when Diogenes quotes from lost works of c. 200 BC what are in fact the earliest references to the Druids known to us. We shall have especial reason to discuss the Alexandrian tradition at greater length when we turn to the Druids' alleged beliefs in immortality and Pythagorean systems.

Before turning to the references to the Druids in the texts of both traditions in detail, we may summarize the argument so far. We begin by remembering that the Greeks and Romans on whose testimony we rely were, like all of us, children of their age, and that it was an age that accepted a supernatural world with which contact might be made by appropriate rituals and verbal formulae; sacrifices and offerings; divination and augury; and, on a lower, rather suspect, scale, magic. However much individual philosophers may have emancipated themselves from superstition, they still lived and wrote in the prevailing climate of thought and feeling. If we then apply the classification made by historians of ideas in respect of civilized concepts of primitive societies, to the texts on the Druids, we find they fall into two groups, characterized respectively by an empirical and an idealizing approach: these, following a recent and quite independent classification obtaining the same results, we may call the Posidonian and the Alexandrian traditions. Stoic philosophy has tinged some of the comments in the first group with idealism and the myth of the Noble Savage, but they are mainly derived from first-hand information on Celtic manners and customs. In the second group idealism takes over to build up a romantic image of barbarian philosophers, and we move from Druids-as-known to Druids-as-wished-for.

THE CELTIC VERNACULAR SOURCES

When we turn to sources on Druids in Celtic literature we enter a world wholly different from that of the classical texts. There is only one group of sources which we can attribute to a pre-Christian origin, and naturally these are the only ones which can be used, since the Druids were representatives of a religion extirpated by Christianity in such areas as Ireland where it had survived Romanization. Our documents are in fact Irish, and belong to the earliest stratum of the literature of that country and language. They constitute, as Kenneth Jackson has recently put it, an 'extraordinary archaic fragment of European literature', reflecting, in the words of another Celtic scholar, Myles Dillon, 'an older world than any other vernacular literature in western Europe'. Their importance has for long been appreciated by students of Celtic language and literature, but they have been less well known to archaeologists, historians and anthropologists, who have perhaps been alarmed and put on their guard by the unscholarly and speculative literature that has gathered around them.

As we saw earlier in this book, we have to deal with a primitive, though not necessarily simple, oral literature in prose, interspersed occasionally with poems and mainly to be divided for our present purpose into hero-tales or epics, and summaries of law codes. It is a literature orally composed and transmitted in a barbaric society, as were the original versions of the Homeric poems or of the Sanskrit *Rig-Veda*. It is not only, in contradistinction to the classical sources, artless and rustic rather than sophisticated and civilized; it also presents Celtic society from within and not from outside. It is not therefore animated by any analytical desire to examine or explain; it is not in any way self-conscious, takes Celtic society for granted, and sees it with approbation through upper-class barbarian eyes.

The archaeological and anthropological importance of the earliest Irish epics, and the manner in which they can be approximately dated, has recently been set out by Jackson. Originally oral compositions designed to be recited for entertainment and edification, and taught by word of mouth to successive generations of bards or story-tellers, the Ulster group of tales can be shown to reflect a pagan world earlier than the introduction of Christianity into Ireland in the fifth century AD, and earlier too than the political situation in the same century. They are prehistoric in the literal sense, and may relate to a period not later than fourth century AD. The general picture of Celtic manners and customs in Ireland presented by these tales is in striking agreement with that of the Posidonian group of classical sources for Gaul, even in points of detail, but the Druids in the vernacular sources do not (as we have seen) hold the place of formal authority that the classical texts imply for an earlier period on the Continent. The clear-cut distinction of function of Druids, bards and seers or diviners is not apparent in either the Irish hero-tales or the law tracts, where Druids share with poets and other men of learning a place in the social hierarchy immediately below the nobility.

To sum up, the Irish vernacular sources, especially the hero-tales, are the product of a primitive, illiterate, heroic society with a warrior-aristocracy, and were composed in accordance with the values and code of manners of this social class. They represent a non-Christian, pagan, world which seems to have been remarkably unaltered in its presentation even though the final redaction and first transference from oral to written form was the work of Christian clerics. In considering this evidence in conjunction with the classical sources we must remember once again that the former represents Ireland, not Gaul; the fourth century AD and not the first or second century BC; and is a barbarian glimpse from within, not a civilized appraisal from outside.

THE NAME 'DRUID'

We may now turn to the information conveyed by the sources in greater detail, and first consider the name of the priesthood itself. In the classical texts it only appears in plural forms, *druidai* in Greek and *druidae* or *druides* in Latin. Aberrant forms like *drasidae* or *drysidae* must result from scribal errors and corruptions in the manuscripts, but Lucan's *dryadae* look as though they have been influenced by the name of the Greek water and tree nymphs, *dryades* in Latin. The forms presuppose a Gaulish *★druvis*, from *★druvids*, but, as we have seen, the word does not actually occur in any Romano-Celtic inscription. In Old Irish the word is *druí*, plural *druid*. There has been much discussion as to the probable etymology of the name, and current opinion tends to concur with those ancient scholars such as Pliny who regarded it as related to the Greek word for an oak-tree, *drus*. The second syllable is regarded as cognate with the Indo-European root *★wid-*, 'to know'. Relationships with such a tree-word would be appropriate enough to a religion with sanctuaries in the deciduous mixed-oak forests of temperate Europe and we shall see how specific association with the oak-tree is attested. The name of the Galatian sanctuary in Asia Minor recorded by Strabo, *Drunemeton*, appears to contain the same first element combined with the Gaulish sanctuary-word *nemeton* discussed in the last chapter.

THE DISTRIBUTION OF DRUIDISM

At its maximum extent before the Roman conquest, the Celtic world as shown by the incidence of La Tène material culture and the distribution of place-names, stretched from the mixed Celtiberians on the west, northwards to the British Isles and the Cologne–Leipzig–Cracow line, to Transylvania and the Balkans in the east, and into Galatian Asia Minor. The classical texts inform us directly of Druids only in Gaul and Britain; Caesar states that there were no Druids in Germany, but the Berne scholiast glosses Lucan's reference with 'Druids: a German people. But there are also Druids who are Gaulish philosophers.' In some of the Alexandrian texts confusion is introduced by the use of the word *Galatai*, which would normally be translated 'Galatians' and applied either to the Celtic peoples of Asia Minor who had migrated there in the third century B C, or to the subsequent Roman province founded in 25 B C. Diogenes Laertius, quoting a late third-century B C source, says the Celts (*Keltoi*) and Galatians (*Galatai*) had seers called *druidae* and *semnotheoi*. We will return to the second word shortly: it is corrupt and its sense is obscure, but the passage could be read as indicating either that the Celts and the 'Galatians' had both Druids and *semnotheoi*, or that they respectively had the one and the other. Diogenes is here giving a list of foreign 'philosophers' (Persian *magi*, Indian Gymnosophists, and so on) and variant versions are given by Clement, who assigns Druids to *Galatai* and philosophers to *Keltoi*; Cyril follows this, and finally in the sixth century Stephen of Byzantium is writing of Druids as the philosophers of the Galatian people (*ethnos Galatikon*). If 'Galatian' is accepted at face value, the place-name *Drunemeton* recently discussed might also be thought to support the existence of Druids in Asia Minor.

But on the other hand an alternative use of 'Galatian' for 'Gaulish' goes back to the Posidonian sources. 'The whole race, which is now called Gaulish or Galatian' (*Gallikon te kai Galatikon*) writes Strabo, who also names both the Gulf of Lions and the Bay of Biscay as 'Galatian' gulfs; Diodorus makes the same alternative use of the adjectives, and distinguishes between Celts in the south and *Galatae* in the north, together named 'Gauls' by the Romans. In the face of this we cannot with any confidence use the Alexandrian sources to indicate the presence of Druids in Celtic Asia Minor, and it would be preferable to regard their use of 'Galatian' as no more than an elegant variation on 'Gaulish'. Essentially then the classical sources show us Gallo-Brittonic Druids, while the vernacular texts naturally depict the local Irish scene.

The position of the Druids in the Celtic social order was an aspect which naturally interested the classical investigators, particularly Posidonius and his followers. As we saw, part of his philosophy involved a belief that in barbarian societies the primal innocence of the Golden Age might linger on, and sages acting as intermediaries between gods and men might be the law-givers and tutors of the community. In the Celtic world the priesthood was in fact a separate, highly respected and impor- tant grade of society, as it was among other contemporary peoples in barbarian Europe, but as it no longer was in Graeco-Roman civilization. This differentiation in social structure was quickly perceived and com- mented upon, and was susceptible of over-emphasis by those looking for ruler-sages among uncivilized peoples. Here philosophical bias might slightly colour the picture; with Caesar, politics could lead to distortion.

In view of a recently expressed opinion that the Druids should not rightly be called priests, or regarded as members of a priesthood, we must briefly take account of nomenclature. Despite Mrs Chadwick's pleading, it seems impossible to use these terms in any reasonable anthropological or historical sense without including Druids with the other named functionaries – bards, diviners and so on – and the doubtless numerous grades whose names have not been preserved, within a Celtic priesthood. A class of learned men, repositories of the traditional wisdom of the tribe whether it concerned the gods or men; the way to write a poem or to construct a calendar; the due rite of sacrifice and the correct inter- pretations of omens – this is a priesthood, and the Druids are an integral part of it, both in the classical and the vernacular sources.

Their position was seen as comparable with the priesthoods of other foreign peoples. Dio Chrysostom in the first century AD equated Druids with Persian *magi*, Egyptian priests, and Indian brahmins, and versions of this list were compiled by the Alexandrians later. Within a vaguer framework, they were seen as representatives of seers, prophets, healers, magicians and diviners: the assorted medicine-men and witch-doctors of the ancient world. Posidonius noted (no doubt rightly, but also surely with some satisfaction) that Druids were 'held in much honour' above the rest of the priesthood, and had authority in peace and war. Seneca tells us that in his Golden Age Posidonius thought his ruler-sages 'restrained the hands of their fellows', and Strabo says that 'in former times' Druids could intervene and stop contending armies from fighting, while Diodorus quotes again their power of calling off hostilities – 'thus even among the most savage barbarians anger yields to wisdom'. Dio Chrysostom makes kings 'become mere ministers of the Druids' will', but this is the golden-mouthed orator inventing his private Golden Age. Caesar on the other hand, for reasons difficult to fathom, stresses the high status of the Druids, putting them equal with the noble class of *equites* among the 'two classes of men of some dignity and importance' in Gaul, gives their functions in details we will discuss later, and stresses their exemption from taxation, military service, and other obligations of 'feudal' type due to the tribal overlords. But drawing on Posidonius, he may well be presenting a state of affairs no longer current in his own time.

In the Posidonian sources the Druids are associated with two other classes of learned and holy men. In Strabo three classes are 'held in special honour'; Bards (*bardoi*) who are singers and poets, *Vates* (*ouateis*) who interpret sacrifices and study natural phenomena, and Druids who are concerned with both natural phenomena and 'moral philosophy'. Diodorus lists Bards, poets chanting both eulogies and satires, Druids, who are 'philosophers and theologians', and *Manteis* who divine from sacrifices and auguries. Ammianus, quoting Timagenes, has Bards again, who 'celebrate the brave deeds of their famous men in epic verse'; Druids who 'are uplifted by searchings into things secret and sublime', profess the immortality of the soul and share Pythagorean beliefs; and *Euhages* who 'strive to explain the high mysteries of nature'. This last name appears to be a corruption of *ouateis*, and by now the loaded terminology of Greek philosophy is beginning to raise the Celtic priesthood into undeserved realms of Noble Savagery. In the sailing-manual attributed to the Pseudo-Scymnus, of c. AD 100, the Celts are attributed with poets and singers, and we know from further references in Diodorus, Ammianus and Lucan that poems commemorating past heroes were a well-known part of their repertoire. Three inscriptions, and a single passage in Book VIII of the *Gallic War* (written by Hirtius) refer to a Gaulish title or office of *gutuater*, which has been interpreted as 'master' or 'father of invocation' or 'the Invoker' and thought to refer to a grade of priesthood, on the grounds that one inscription records a magistrate and a priest of the Celtic deity Moltinus who was also *gutuater martis*. The other inscriptions are to persons of unknown status, to a Celtic nobleman, and to a Romano-Celtic colonial prefect, so that the relationship of the title to the Celtic social order remains ambiguous. The *semnotheoi* already mentioned are even more obscure, whatever the uncorrupted form of the word may have been, which seems to have conveyed some sense of 'reverence to the gods'.

Perhaps no great importance should be attached to these named classes within the priesthood, no greater at least than one would, with very little knowledge of Hinduism, give to a few comments from eighteenth-century Englishmen in India mentioning the names of *brahmin, fakir* and *guru*. Certainly the status of what continued to be called a Druid became debased and vague in the later texts. Whatever the dubious authority of the fourth-century *Scriptores Historiae Augustae*, the writers represented popular feeling, proceeding 'on ordinary journalistic lines' with 'the usual escape into oracles' and mysteries, and its stories of female Druids show the low position to which the *mulier dryas* had fallen, now no more than a Gaulish spae-wife keeping an inn and telling Diocletian's fortune as he crosses her palm with silver in paying his bill.

We have seen the status of the Druid in early Irish law, among the 'men of art' immediately below the nobility, but it is likely that exceptionally they could themselves be of high rank, for in the earliest hero-tales Conchobar, chieftain of Ulster, has the Druid Cathbad as his father, who was the leader of a warrior-band when young and in later life is his son's Druid and adviser. He teaches his pupils the traditional learning, and also assists in the rites attending on the young warriors' taking arms. With sons of the nobility entering for instruction into the priesthood, as the classical and vernacular texts demonstrate, its status must always have been high. A classic problem is that of the Aeduan chieftain Diviciacus, presented by Caesar as a soldier and statesmen, but by Cicero as a Druid. The grave uncertainty as to whether Diviciacus could speak adequate Latin at any time of his career throws doubts both on Cicero's report of his philosophical views, and on the nature of the Noble Savage speech which, leaning picturesquely on his long Celtic shield, he is reported to have addressed to the Roman senate about 60 B C. The episode in the early Irish epic where 'druids, poets, satirists and cheek-blisterers' are sent to taunt a warrior into taking up arms recalls the satirical poets associated with Druids by Diodorus.

ORGANIZATION, RECRUITMENT AND TEACHING

75, 76   Caesar is our only authority for Druidic organization under a single pontiff in Gaul. 'The Druids,' he wrote, 'have one at their head who holds chief authority among them. When he dies, either the highest in honour among the others succeeds, or if some are on an equal footing they contend for leadership by a vote of the Druids, but sometimes even in arms.' This statement, unsupported by any other writer, naturally raises the suspicion that a situation may have been exaggerated or even invented by Caesar in a process of persuading his readers of the nation-wide political power of a priesthood whose repugnant practices of human sacrifice he later stresses: such an uncivilized anti-Roman faction would obviously merit opposition and liquidation. He then goes on to describe annual meetings of a Druid assembly in a sacred place (*in loco consecrato*) in the tribal territory of the Carnutes, believed to be the 'centre of all Gaul'.

The existence of such a meeting would receive support from the council of 300 elected from the three tribes constituting the Galatians (the Tectosages, the Trocmi and the Tolistobogii), which met to judge cases of bloodshed in the *Drunemeton* sanctuary in Asia Minor. It does however raise the question as to how much, among the totality of the tribes of Gaul, there could be any concept of Gaulish 'nationality'. For propaganda purposes, it was desirable for Caesar to give such an impression, and he certainly lets it be implied that he was conquering *Gallia omnis*, not merely *Gallia comata*, and that *Gallia* is synonymous with *Celtica*. There may have been some wild and vague idea of a unity beyond the shifting coalition of a few tribes in the minds of exceptional
77   Gauls like Dumnorix or Vercingetorix, but we cannot use as evidence of this the fictitious patriotic speeches attributed to them in their role of Noble Savages, any more than we can with Diviciacus. Such speeches were part of the stock-in-trade of ancient historiography, and of an

75 Contemporary portrait of Julius Caesar on a bronze *denarius*.

honourable tradition. 'I have put into the mouths of each speaker senti-
ments proper to the occasion, expressed as I thought him likely to
express them,' wrote Thucydides, and in the hands of Caesar, 'a master
of rearrangement, emphasis, omission, skilfully directed to his own
political aim', it was an obvious device to enhance in the eyes of his
readers the Celtic Peril he was so valiantly combating.

The holy place believed to be the centre of Gaul has the ring of truth, for
as Eliade has stressed, such sacred centres can be many, each with its own
mystical validity, and the *omphalos* at Delphi is merely one of the most
famous. Celtic names embodying the 'middle' element, like *Medionemeton* and *Mediolanum* (Milan) may have enshrined the same concept.
But apart from the reference in Caesar we have no other recorded meeting-
place of the Druids.

As we saw when discussing the archaeological evidence for Celtic
sanctuaries or temples, the absence of formal buildings for religious
purposes struck the classical world as peculiar, as did the setting of the
locus consecratus away from the village or *oppidum*, rather than within its

IULIUS CÆSAR

The first Roman that Discovered and Invaded Brittain.

W. Dolle sc:

76 Engraving of Julius Caesar by W. Dolle.

77 (*opposite*) A 'Noble Savage' speech by the British chieftain Caractacus as given by Henry Rowlands in his *Mona Antiqua Restaurata*, 1723.

THE
SPEECH
OF
CARACTACUS.

When *CARACTACUS*, with a great Train of his Countrymen and Family, was brought in Chains before the Emperour, he spake (says *Tacitus*) to' this purpose, as he stood before *Cæsar's* Tribunal.

IF the Moderation of my Mind in *Prosperity* had been answerable to my *Quality* and *Fortune*, I might have come a Friend *rather than a* Captive *into this City, and you without dishonour might have confederated with me, Royally descended, and then at the Head of many Nations. As my State at present is disgraceful; so yours is honourable and glorious: I had Horses, Men, Arms and Riches; why then is it strange I should unwillingly part with them? But since your Power and Empire must be Universal, we of course among all others, must be Subject: If I had forthwith yielded, neither my Fortune nor your Glory had been so eminent in the World: My Grave would have bury'd the Memory of it, as well as me: Whereas if you suffer me to live now, your Clemency will live in me for ever, as an Example to after Ages.*

NOW, what so brief, and together so full and transcendently surprising, as the words of this brave Heroick Person (probably spoke in his own *British* Tongue, and interpreted to the Noble Audience?) his Address and Comportment, his strong Sense and Courage, what are they, but so many Advocates for our Country's Reputation, so

many

bounds. Instead, the sanctuary was a lonely forest clearing, perhaps delimited by an earthwork or palisade enclosure; a *nemeton*. The association of Druids and oak-trees underline this; Pliny in his account of the ritual gathering of the mistletoe set a specific religious ceremony in such a woodland scene. Lucan, writing of the Druids, exclaims: 'The innermost glades of far-off forests are your abode,' and this is echoed by his commentators in the Berne manuscript. The teaching of young men next to be described again took place in such a forest setting, appropriate to the rural and uncentralized character of Celtic religion.

Two texts in the Posidonian group give us specific information on the recruitment and instruction of novitiates in Druid doctrine, Pomponius Mela and Caesar respectively. The former is less disjointed in his Posidonian borrowings; the Druids, he says, 'teach many things to the nobles of Gaul in a course of instruction, lasting as long as 20 years, meeting in secret in a cave or *in abditis saltibus*', which could be translated as 'remote woods' or 'valleys'. Caesar says that 'a large number of young men flock to them for training', and then later adds that the studies could last 20 years and were orally transmitted: 'it is said they commit to memory large amounts of poetry' (*magnum numerum versuum*). To the classical world, accustomed to formal or public teaching in cities, scholars at the feet of a recluse among the woods was an unfamiliar concept, though it would not have been strange to a contemporary Hindu or Buddhist, nor to an Early Christian Irish monk. The Celtic sanctuary too, as we saw, was essentially in a forest clearing. Oral teaching and learning by heart of mnemonic verses was again part of the ancient tradition of non-literate societies from India to Ireland, where the early laws were preserved 'by the joint memory of the ancients, the transmission from one ear to another, the chanting of the poets'. The 20-year period may merely be a way of expressing a long duration of time, but it may conceivably be a reference to a 19-year calendrical cycle which as we shall see was probably known to the Celts as well as to other peoples in antiquity.

Caesar also states of Druid teaching that 'it is thought that this system of training was invented in Britain and taken over from there to Gaul, and at the present time diligent students of the matter mostly travel there to study it.' This unsupported statement may represent a genuine Celtic belief current at the time, and Jackson has drawn attention to an early Irish reference to a *fili* returning from study of the craft in Britain. Cathbad, the Druid in the early Irish tales, is depicted as teaching a class of young noblemen, 100 in one instance, and eight in another. Bards and *filid* (a name originally meaning 'seers') were also taught in special schools in ancient Ireland, with oral tuition and memorizing lasting from seven to twelve years: such schools continued in Ireland to the seventeenth and in Gaelic Scotland to the beginning of the eighteenth century.

FUNCTIONS AND ACTIVITIES

As a high-ranking class of learned, non-combatant, respected and holy men within a barbarian society of heroic type the Druids, as we saw, can only be regarded as members of a priesthood together with the bards, seers or diviners. Ethnographical parallels could easily be quoted: the *arioi* of Tahiti must have appeared to the first European invaders of that island very much as the Druids did to the classical world, even to their practice of human sacrifice. From the Posidonian sources especially we can perceive some at least of the main duties and activities of the Druids within the general hierarchy. There seems to have been no over-lapping with the *bardoi*, to whom are consistently attributed the task of poetic composition, whether eulogy or satire, as well as the declamation or singing of these poems for purposes of ceremonial or entertainment. There seems however a slight ambivalence between the functions of the Druids and of the *vates* or *manteis*, the diviners and seers, in some of the texts. Cicero, specifically writing on divination, stated that Diviciacus as a Druid made prophetic utterances from auguries and omens (*partim auguriis, partim coniectura*); Dio Chrysostom makes the Druids to be con-cerned with divination, and Hippolytus in the third century classes them as 'prophets and prognosticators' because they can foretell certain events by mathematical computations, a point we must return to.

Otherwise, certain functions are clearly enough assigned to the Druids. In the first place they are concerned with knowledge and learning in matters sacred and profane and with the transmission of this know-ledge to novitiates. Pomponius Mela calls them 'professors of wisdom' (*magistri sapientiae*), and we have seen how this teaching was carried out and will discuss the nature of their knowledge in another section, but it must not be forgotten how the Greek and Latin philosophical termino-logy may give a false picture of its profundity. The Druids were awarded (as again we saw) the stock phrase 'the most just of men', but they do in fact seem to have wielded considerable juridical power, at least in Caesar's account. Strabo is careful to say that only 'in former times' did they arbitrate in war and could stop a battle (and in Diodorus it appears that the bards could also act in this way) but adds that now they are 'entrusted with the decisions of cases affecting either individuals or the public' and 'murder cases have been mostly entrusted' to them. Caesar in his version of the same passage of Posidonius emphasizes their wide-spread power in Gaul, their authority in nearly all civil and criminal cases as well as in questions of property and boundaries, and their annual judgement of disputes under the chief Druid. He also adds that they could excommunicate from attendance at sacrifices an individual or a tribe who did not accept their rulings, thus rendering them outcasts without religious or legal status. The well-known scene in Tacitus of the con-frontation of Druids and the Roman army in Anglesey shows that ritual cursing was another means of invoking divine wrath when needed.

Our information on Druid ceremonies mainly centres on sacrifice, and is contained in the Posidonian sources and in Pliny. Strabo writes in the past tense of 'sacrifices and divinations that are opposed to our usage', since suppressed by the Romans, and describes how a human victim was stabbed in the back, and omens deduced from his death-throes. Diodorus gives a slightly variant version of the same rite. Other forms of human sacrifice detailed by Strabo included shooting to death by arrows, or by impaling, and the holocaust of human and animal victims alike in a huge wickerwork figure (*kolosson*). Caesar likewise describes these great figures (*immani magnitudine simulacra*) whose limbs were filled with living men and set on fire. This strange rite, which has caught the imagination of all who subsequently wrote on Druids, remains unexplained and unparalleled. The St Sebastian-like death by arrows seems to indicate the ritual use of a weapon not in normal use, for archery was not practised in Celtic warfare, and probably hardly at all: in the vernacular texts of the earliest phase bows and arrows are not mentioned, and the Irish names for these are respectively Norse and Latin loan-words.

78

Pliny gives us the only detailed account of a Druid ceremony. This was determined by observing the growth of mistletoe on an oak tree, a circumstance of rare occurrence. The time chosen for the subsequent rite was the sixth day of the moon, and preparations were made for a feast and a sacrifice of two white bulls. A Druid in a white robe climbed the tree and cut with a golden sickle (*falce aurea demetit*) the branch of mistletoe, which was caught as it fell on a white cloak. The bulls were then sacrificed. The golden sickle is inexplicable, and if it really existed would have been useless to cut the tough stem of mistletoe: gilded bronze is more likely. Pliny's account of the ritual necessity of gathering the plant *samolus* left-handed and fasting, and of plucking *selago* without using an iron knife, barefoot and with the right hand through the left sleeve of a white tunic, are performances of private magic rather than corporate ceremonial.

The aspect of Druid function that has been found most embarrassing to certain apologists is their association with human sacrifice. Animal sacrifices are involved in Pliny's description of the cutting of the mistletoe from an oak-tree as we have just seen. Diodorus assigns animal and human sacrifice to the seers (*manteis*); Strabo classes the equivalent *vates* as interpreters of sacrifices in general, but does not specify the precise practitioners among the hierarchy who actually carried out the animal and human holocausts in wicker figures. Caesar, who of course does not divide the priesthood, follows the Posidonius in the same manner as Strabo by stating that Druids were essential participants in such sacrifices, even if they did not carry out the murder of the victims with their own hands. He specifically states in addition that one of their main functions was to 'look after public and private sacrifice'. Tacitus is specific on the British Druids: 'they deemed it indeed a duty to cover their altars with the blood of captives and to consult their deities through human entrails.' To such passages we must add the recurrent references to human sacrifice among Gauls and Celts from the third century BC to Cicero, Dionysius of Halicarnassus and Pomponius Mela (taken up and repeated by early Church fathers such as Tertullian, Augustine and Lactantius as examples of pagan iniquities), and to Roman proscriptions instanced later.

It is hardly realistic to exculpate the Druids from participation, probably active, in both the beliefs and practices involved in human

78 The Wicker Image: engraving from Aylett Sammes, *Britannia Antiqua Illustrata*, 1676. Sammes freely translates Caesar's text (BG VI. 16) describing human sacrifices in *immani magnitudine simulacra*, adding 'the strangeness of which Custome, I have here thought not amiss to represent the view'.

sacrifice (which after all had only been brought to an end in the civilized Roman world in the early first century B C). The Druids were the wise men of barbarian Celtic society, and Celtic religion was their religion, with all its crudities. It is sheer romanticism and a capitulation to the myth of the Noble Savage to imagine that they stood by the sacrifices in duty bound, but with disapproval in their faces and elevated thoughts in their minds. Mention of human sacrifice is omitted by the later writers of the Alexandrian tradition, but here soft primitivism and idealization have taken over. In sum, in the classical sources in the Posidonian group, on which we may place most reliance, the Druids appear to have three main functions. In the first place they are the repositories of the traditional lore and knowledge of the tribe, whether of the gods, the cosmos and the other-world, or of the corpus of customary law and such practical skills as calendrical expertise. This body of knowledge was preserved in oral tradition (and probably mainly in verse form for mnemonic reasons) and continuity achieved by explicit instruction to the younger generation entering the priesthood. The Druids' second function in Gaul was the practical application of their learning in law and to the administration of justice, though how this power operated side-by-side with that of the tribal chief or the *vergobretos* is nowhere explained. Finally, the Druids supervised sacrifices and religious ceremonies in general, in which they and other functionaries (for instance *vates* or *manteis*) participated. Any divinatory powers they were believed to exercise would fall quite appropriately within their general priestly duties.

In the Irish sources the functions of the Druids are less well defined and particularized. They appear as confidential advisers to the chiefs on omens and auguries, or lucky and unlucky days, and they instruct the young warriors of the tribe. They practice magic to confuse or confound the enemy, but it seems probable that it is precisely in the sphere of the Druids' religious activities that the Christian redaction of the hero-tales would make the most severe excisions, and the texts are almost wholly uninformative on this aspect.

THE NATURE OF THE DRUIDS' KNOWLEDGE:
THE SUPERNATURAL

In estimating the scope and nature of the Celtic traditional lore believed to be possessed by the Druids we may conveniently divide our available information into two groups, one relating to metaphysical speculation and beliefs about the supernatural, and the other dealing with practical knowledge, including that involved in the construction of a calendar. In the first group ideas about human immortality play a large part, which naturally struck the imaginations of the Greek and Roman writers, and were particularly elaborated by the Alexandrian school.

Beginning with the Posidonian and allied sources, and remembering the loaded terminology of classical philosophy, we find the following statements about supernatural beliefs, excluding for the moment the beliefs about immortality, to be discussed separately. The Druids in Diodorus are 'philosophers and theologians', 'skilled in the divine nature' and able to communicate with the gods. Strabo notes not only their practical knowledge of natural phenomena, but their pursuit of 'moral philosophy'. Caesar stresses this dual fund of knowledge, with their religious beliefs elaborated into 'the powers and spheres of action of the immortal gods', adding in another place a specific belief, that the Gauls 'all assert their descent from Dis Pater'. Lucan addresses the Druids in a very elliptical passage which may be rendered: 'To you alone is given knowledge of the gods and heavenly powers – either this, or you only have not this knowledge.' Ammianus, quoting Timagenes with an idealizing bias, makes the Druids investigate 'problems of things secret and sublime' (which is vague enough), while Mela simply says they profess to know the will of the gods (*quid dii velint*), which really seems to sum up all the foregoing comments. In the Alexandrian sources the Druids become formidable philosophers, on a footing with those of other nations, as a part of the process of idealization in a mood of soft primitivism. As Camille Jullian put it, 'With the propensity of the ancients for hasty generalizations, the Druids could appear simultaneously as the most bloodthirsty and the most wise of priesthoods, although all the evidence implies that their ritual and beliefs were banality itself.'

THE BELIEF IN IMMORTALITY

The item of Druidic belief which struck the classical writers most forcibly was that of literal personal immortality. In Posidonius as quoted by Diodorus, the Celts held that 'the souls of men are immortal, and that after a definite number of years they live a second life when the soul passes to another body'. Strabo puts this in the form of a belief of the Druids 'as well as other authorities' that 'men's souls and the universe are indestructible, although at times fire and water may prevail'. Caesar makes the chief point of doctrine 'that souls do not suffer death, but after death pass from the one to the other', *ab aliis . . . transire ad alios*. Ammianus quotes Timagenes to the effect that the Druids 'with grand contempt for mortal lot . . . professed the immortality of the soul', while Mela names as the best-known dogma of the Druids 'that souls are eternal and there is another life in the infernal regions', and like Caesar rationalizes this as an incentive to pointless bravery in war. Lucan, in the rhetorical address to the Druids already quoted goes on:

> 'But you assure us, no ghosts seek the
> silent kingdom of Erebus, nor the pallid depths of Dis' realm, but with
> a new body the spirit reigns in another world – if we understand your
> hymns death's halfway through a long life.'

Diodorus, Ammianus and Valerius Maximus associate the belief in immortality with the Pythagorean theory of metempsychosis, equating the Celtic doctrine with the 'belief of Pythagoras' or idealizing this by making Druids 'members of the intimate fellowship of the Pythagorean faith'. This leads us to the Alexandrian sources, where Hippolytus not only makes the Druids to have 'profoundly examined the Pythagorean faith' but to have been instructed in it by the mythical Thracian Zalmoxis, said to have been a pupil of Pythagoras himself. With such writers as Clement and Cyril we are in a world where the Druids are not only wholly Pythagorean, but where the invention of that school of philosophy is even attributed to them. We are hardly surprised to find too that Anacharsis the Scythian sage, and the vegetarian Hyperboreans, as well as Zalmoxis, are all brought together in this dream-world of barbarian philosophers.

It has been pointed out on more than one occasion that the Celtic doctrine of immortality, as set out in the sources just quoted, is not in fact Pythagorean in content at all, in that it does not imply a belief in the transmigration of souls through all living things – 'that the soul of our grandam might haply inhabit a bird' – but only a naive. literal and vivid re-living of an exact counterpart of earthly life beyond the grave. Despite the Greek influence on Celtic culture from the time of Pythagoras (in what was archaeologically the Hallstatt D phase of barbarian Europe), we need hardly look to outside sources for this simple concept, corroborated not only by the tales of the classical writers, such as that of Celts offering to pay off debts in the after-life, and by the inferences to be drawn from the earlier Irish literature, but also by the archaeological evidence discussed in chapter II. What is surely significant is the very real contrast between the Celtic and the classical vision of eternity and the after-life, which would render the former so strange as to be necessary of explanation in some familiar philosophical terms: this is the contrast explicitly stressed by Lucan, though in Pythagorean terms.

Behind the classical concepts of the other-world lay earlier Oriental beliefs, such as the sinister Dark House of Death in Sumerian mythology, where the dead crouch like bedraggled birds in dust and blackness. For the Greeks, death was 'an inevitable relegation to a loathly underworld of darkness and silence, a land of gloomy caverns and desolate marshes, where the very gods were livid and devoid of pulsing life; the Romans, influenced by Etruscan beliefs, took a grimmer and more lurid view.' How contrasted, Richmond went on to say, was the naive reality implicit in for instance the Romano-Batavian stone sarcophagus from 79 Simpelveld of the third century AD, carved inside with a complete bas-relief rendering of the deceased's household furniture and belongings, an unambiguous 'conception of individual survival, into a world which is a continuation or a projection of that with which such believers were already familiar'. But it was unfamiliar to the classical world, which seems to have felt that the idea of transference from one life in the living body to an identical life in an immaterial one beyond the grave was so extraordinary as to demand an explanation, which could be done only by bringing it in some way within the framework of its own philosophical systems. The Pythagorean myth seemed to provide the only approximation, however vague, and by equating Celtic belief with this

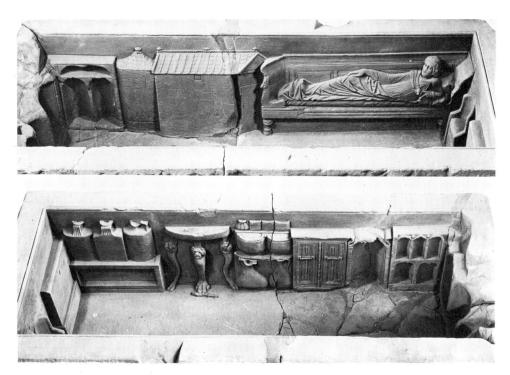

79 Stone sarcophagus of a Batavian lady of the third century AD from Simpelveld, Netherlands, showing internal furnishings of her house.

it could be brought into a satisfactory tidy relationship with civilized systems of thought, and of course enhance the *mystique* of Druid philosophy. It was a simple belief, appropriate to the society which held it. Alexander Pope summed it up in another primitive context when he wrote:

> 'Go, like the Indian, in another life,
> Expect thy dog, thy bottle and thy wife.'

PRACTICAL KNOWLEDGE

There is interesting evidence for an important branch of practical knowledge among the Druids, that of astronomy and calendrical computations. We saw that Strabo not only mentions the Druids' knowledge of moral philosophy but of *physiologia* or natural science, and the same word is used by Cicero of Diviciacus, who, he said, 'claimed to have that knowledge of nature that the Greeks call *physiologia*'. Caesar amplifies this as usual, attributing to the Druids 'much knowledge of the stars and their motion, of the size of the world and of the earth, of natural philosophy'; Mela, probably like Caesar drawing on Posidonius, gives this as 'the size and shape of the world, the movements of the heavens and of the stars'. Hippolytus attributes the status of the Druids as prophets to the fact 'they can foretell certain events by the Pythagorean reckoning and calculations'. From Caesar we know the Celts counted by nights and not days 'and in reckoning birthdays and the new moon and new year their unit of reckoning is the night followed by the day'. Pliny ascribes this form of time-measuring specifically to the Druids, 'for it is by the moon that they measure their months and years and also their "ages" (*saeculi*) of 30 years'.

Clearly this amounts to a considerable competence in calendrical skill, which is epigraphically corroborated by a remarkable document, the Coligny Calendar. This is the now fragmentary remains of a great bronze plate, five feet by three feet six inches, engraved with a calendar of 62 consecutive lunar months, with two 'intercalary' months, found at Coligny near Bourg-en-Bresse (Ain), and probably Augustan in date. The lettering and numerals are Roman, the language Gaulish, and many of the words are abbreviated. It is divided into half-months, reckons by nights, and marks lucky and unlucky days. In basic construction it represents an adjustment of the lunar to the solar year by the insertion of the 'intercalary' months of 30 days at $2\frac{1}{2}$- and 3-year intervals alternately, and in some details reflects Greek rather than Roman calendrical practice. Its scheme might be related to a major 30-year cycle of the type indicated by Pliny, but more plausibly to the 19-year cycle known in Babylonian and Greek mathematics, and in the latter instance associated with the name of Meton, who supported its adoption in Athens, where however it was only employed between 338 and 290 B C. Hecateus attributed a knowledge of this same cycle to the Hyperboreans which he located in the British Isles. Its practical significance lies in the fact that 19 solar years are (within about half a day) the equivalent of 235 lunar months: with this knowledge it is possible to add extra months as required in a regular cycle, and so reconcile the solar and lunar calendars.

The Celts were not alone in barbarian Europe in the possession of such astronomical skill. The recent excavations of the very remarkable circular calendrical monuments in stone and wood in the Dacian capital of Sarmizegetusa in what is now Romania, destroyed by the Romans, gives archaeological evidence for considerable local astronomical knowledge in the first century B C. Such calendrical expertise is in fact common to many relatively barbarian societies. Jordanes (or his source, Cassiodorus) describes in the sixth century A D the activities of a semi-legendary Dicineus among the Getae in the first century B C, who taught them both natural and moral philosophy, 'the courses of the twelve signs and of the planets passing through them, and the whole of astronomy' as well as 'the names of the three hundred and fifty-six stars'. By his wisdom, Dicineus 'gained marvellous repute among them'; he trained novitiates 'of noblest birth and superior wisdom and taught them theology, bidding them worship certain divinities and holy places', and indeed 'ruled not only the common men but their kings'. Dicineus in fact is an excellent example of the barbarian priest skilled in calendrical expertise, later elevated to the mythical status of a philosopher-king. As we have seen, this description of a Getic priest might equally well have been applied to a Celtic Druid.

'The observation of the calendar,' writes Nilsson, 'is a special occupation which is placed in the hands of specially experienced and gifted men. . . . Behind the calendar stand in particular the priests.' Elaborate computations do not necessarily involve apparatus or even the writing of figures. Among the Tamil calendar-makers of South India in the last century the calculation of eclipses was done by arranging shells or pebbles on the ground in such a way as to recall to the mind of the operator the necessary algorithm, or steps in the process. One man, who 'did not understand a word of the theories of Hindu mathematics, but was endowed with a retentive memory, which enabled him to arrange very distinctly his operations in his mind, and on the ground' predicted by such methods a lunar eclipse in 1825 within four minutes of its true time. It is quite conceivable that some elements of Greek mathematics found their way into the Celtic world through the Massaliot contacts from c. 600 BC, and these would support the statement of Hippolytus about 'Pythagorean' calculations, even if they were not literally these in fact. Indeed it may be that any Pythagorean doctrine acquired by the Druids is less likely to have been concerned with the esoteric mysteries of transmigration of souls, than with such mundane affairs as the value of the square on the hypotenuse of a right-angled triangle.

MAGIC AND GNOMIC WISDOM

Under this heading we may conveniently set a few pieces of information on the Druids which hardly fit into the foregoing sections. Pliny's stories about the charms wrought by the Druids with mistletoe, *selago* and *samolus*, may well be associated with a genuine empirical knowledge of herbs and simples, but also fit in with the vague attributions of magic echoed by more than one source. The remaining Druid story in Pliny relates to a magic egg, the *anguinum*, reputedly made by the spittle and secretions of angry snakes, esteemed by the Druids and believed to 'ensure success in law-courts and a favourable reception by princes'. Now Pliny had been shown an *anguinum*: 'it was round, and about as large as a smallish apple; the shell was cartilaginous and pocked like the arms of a polypus.' A sea-urchin, denuded of its spines and fresh or fossil, has been suggested, but unconvincingly, since this would surely have been recognized for what it was by Pliny, and does not really accord with the description. A preferable alternative would be the ball of agglomerated empty egg-cases of a Whelk (*Buccinum*), which has a parchment-like *80* texture and a nodulated surface, for since *Buccinum* is a genus confined to Atlantic and northern waters, its egg-cases, common enough objects on a North Gaulish or British beach, might be quite unfamiliar to a Mediterranean naturalist, and so capable of being endowed for him with magic powers.

There are two pieces of Celtic gnomic or proverbial wisdom recorded by the classical writers, and one attributed specifically to the Druids, that deserve comment here. Diogenes Laertius attributes to 'Gymnosophists and Druids' certain 'riddles and dark sayings', 'teaching that the gods

80 Ball of egg capsules of the Whelk (*Buccinum undetum*), slightly larger than life, and perhaps what Pliny was told was an *anguinum*, or Druidic magic egg.

must be worshipped, and no evil done, and manly behaviour maintained'. This is a statement in typically Celtic triadic form, and it is interesting to find what must be another version of it in an Irish tale, *The Colloquy of the Elders*, which dates from the end of the twelfth century, but may incorporate earlier material. Here St Patrick talks to one of the old pagan Celtic heroes, Caelte, and asks him: 'Who or what was it that maintained you so in your life?'; to which comes the answer, 'Truth that was in our hearts, and strength in our arms, and fulfilment in our tongues' – essentially the same three qualities in slightly different order.

The other Celtic proverbial statement occurring in both groups of sources was detected by Jackson. He pointed out that Strabo and Arrian reported that certain Celts had said to Alexander that they feared nothing, unless the heavens might fall on them, and Aristotle says that a very rash man fears neither earthquakes nor waves 'as they say of the Celts'. When we turn to the Irish vernacular texts we find the chief's bodyguard in a final engagement swearing to stand firm 'though the earth should split under us and the sky above on us'. It looks, however, as though this may be a proverbial saying of wider distribution in the ancient world. There is a line in the *Iliad* – 'Thus shall a man speak: then let the wide earth open to take me' – which is reminiscent of half the phrase, but more apposite is a sentence in one of the earliest inscriptions in the Turkic language, of the eighth century AD, on the Orkhon River south of Lake Baikal – 'So long as the heaven above and the earth below have not opened, O Turkish people, who can destroy your rule?' Here we may have an extraordinarily widespread proverbial phrase attested in widely differing contexts, places and cultures, one being the Celtic world of the Druids.

THE END OF THE DRUIDS IN GAUL AND BRITAIN

As is well known, the Druids and the religion they represented were, by the early first century AD, made the object of successive measures of repression by the Roman authorities. Augustus, according to Suetonius, took action to prohibit *religio druidarum* to those who had become Roman citizens; Pliny relates how under Tiberius a decree of the senate was issued against the Gaulish Druids 'and all that kind of diviners and healers' (*et hoc genus vatum medicorumque*). And then Suetonius again states that Claudius in AD 54 'completely abolished the barbarous and inhuman religion of the Druids in Gaul'. The name 'druid' in the debased sense of a magician or prophet lingered on, as the stories about the prophecies made by female Druids to Alexander Severus, Aurelian and Diocletian in the *Historia Augusta* show. It was also remembered in a perhaps more honourable sense by Ausonius in the fourth century, who describes a worthy of his time as 'sprung from the stock of the Druids of Bayeux'.

After his mention of the Tiberian decree, Pliny goes on 'but why mention all this about a practice that has crossed the Ocean and penetrated the utmost parts of the earth? At the present day (*hodie*) Britain is still fascinated by magic, and performs its rites with so much ceremony that it almost seems as though it was she who imparted the cult to the Persians.' Pliny was revising his book up to the time of his death in the eruption of Vesuvius in AD 79, but must here refer to a time early or midway in the first century. The action against the Druids of Tiberius (who died in AD 37) would not have affected Britain, the conquest of which was not begun until AD 43, and the Claudian abolition appears only to have applied to Gaul. Tacitus writing of British Druids is describing events of AD 61, and implies that the religion was being stamped out at that time.

The reasons for these legislative measures have been a matter of discussion. One view, supported particularly by Last, holds that it was the intolerable barbarities of Celtic human sacrifice that shocked Roman sensibility and brought about forcible suppression. Human sacrifice in the Roman world had been stamped out by a senate decree of 97 BC, and Augustus and Tiberius had both sought to mitigate the bestialities of the gladiatorial shows. 'What Rome attacked in Gaul was barbarism, especially as manifested in rites of human sacrifice . . . the Romans counted the suppression of savagery as part of their service to mankind.'

This seems a reasonable interpretation of the evidence, but an alternative has been put forward, that Roman opposition arose because (in Collingwood's words) 'Celtic religion wore an intolerant nationalistic shape in the form of Druidism'; Mrs Chadwick has in part endorsed this view. However, she draws attention to the fact that, despite his over-emphasis of Druidic power in his Posidonian borrowings, 'the druids were never at any point during Caesar's campaign a formidable force in Gaulish politics'. De Witt, who developed this theme, makes the convincing point that Caesar's source represents an out-of-date state of affairs, at variance with the absence of any mention of Druids in the actual narrative of the campaigns. To this may be added the point made earlier in this chapter, that the idea of Gaulish 'nationalism' may be a fiction and an anachronism, obtained by projecting into the ancient barbarian world of petty tribal and familial units the modern concept of the unified national state. One wonders what 'national' reality lay behind the Arvernian league at the eve of the conquest of the Province in 121 BC, or behind any other nominal coalition in the Celtic world. But one must also remember that Last's paper was written immediately after the 1939–45 war in a climate of feeling in which suppression of a Gaulish *resistance* could hardly, in view of then recent events, be other than deplored, and Last wished Rome to be in the right.

There seems no reason not to accept the evidence for punitive action against human sacrifice and the attendant barbarities of Celtic religion, and it is likely that wider issues were involved. Without inventing a resistance movement, we can recognize in the very pattern and texture of early Celtic society an incompatibility with Roman mores, exacerbated by certain of its essential components. The classical and vernacular evidence, as we have seen, reveals a learned class including jurists, poets, and holy men, which the Irish sources would suggest were, like other craftsmen, an itinerant and mobile element in the population, as well as being a fundamental part of the social order. Such mobility would run counter to the static agricultural and urban pattern of a Roman province, and in the Druids, embodying myth and ritual, poetry and law, the essentially un-Roman Celtic tradition was concentrated.

We should probably not be far off the mark if we compared Roman policy towards Gauls and Britain with that of the Elizabethan English towards the Irish of the sixteenth century, who had conserved so many features of their prehistoric Celtic past. It was not only a pastoral society, opposed to the English sedentary agriculture of the day, that had to be made stable, but more dangerous still were the travelling men who embodied the traditions of that society. 'The resident officials in Ireland,' Professor Quinn has written, 'gave considerable thought to the wiping-out of the two significant and overlapping elements in Irish society, the travelling craftsmen, messengers and entertainers, and the learned class of brehons [jurists] and poets. . . . This would have torn asunder significant parts of the structure of Irish society, more particularly by eliminating the jurists – the poets were more difficult to silence.' But the turn of 'the rhymers' was soon to come, and their attempted extirpation together with the eradication of the rest of the indigenous and incompatible culture were carried out with savage barbarism by such gallant gentlemen as Sir Humphrey Gilbert.

Roman civilization and Celtic barbarism were from the first opposed in structure and temper. The Druids 'were doomed in the natural course of things to lose their prestige, and even their identity' with the Romanization of Gaul and Britain, as were the *arioi* of Tahiti when their own barbarian culture was forcibly disrupted by the English missionaries in the 1790's. Druids were a casualty in the larger struggle resulting from what Professor Alfoldi called the 'Moral Barrier' between two irreconcilable cultures – 'the fundamental antithesis between civilized mankind under Roman rule and the world of barbarians on its outskirts' with its 'prevalence of vehement instincts and of bestial passions' expressed in such activities as human sacrifice. Druids, bards, seers and the rest had no place in the new Romano-Celtic world which was coming into being in the provinces of the Empire.

HISTOIRE DE
L'ESTAT ET
REPVBLIQVE · DES
DRVIDES, EVBAGES, SAR-
RONIDES, BARDES, VACIES, AN-
ciens François , Gouuerneurs des païs de la
Gaule, depuis le deluge vniuerfel , iufques à la
venuë de Iefus-Chrift en ce monde.

*Compris en deux liures , contenants leurs Loix,
Police, Ordonnances & couftumes, tant en
l'eftat Ecclefiaftique que Seculier.*

Efcrit nouuellement en François.

A PARIS,
Chez IEAN PARANT, ruë
S. Iacques.
1585.
AVEC PRIVILEGE DV ROY.

81 Title-page of Noel Taillepied, *Histoire de l'Estat et Republique des Druides . . .* , 1585.

Chapter Four

THE ROMANTIC IMAGE

THE REDISCOVERY OF DRUIDS

With the break-up of the ancient world and the rise of medieval Christendom in Western Europe, knowledge of the Druids was lost; submerged in a past, forgotten because it had become irrelevant. The pagan past of Gaul or Britain had no significance for the story of mankind's Fall and Redemption; there was only one past relevant and necessary to the Christian, and that was contained in the uniquely authoritative pages of the Old and New Testaments. The pagan poets might be quoted, usually at second-hand from anthologies, or elevated, like Virgil, to magical status, or assorted scraps of Greek and Latin lore would be swept up in the capacious nets of the encyclopaedists like Isidore of Seville, but Celts and Germans, Druids and Bards, had no status as subjects of enquiry, simply because they could have no place in the historical world-picture of the medieval scholar.

The rediscovery of Druids came, incidentally and accidentally, with the change in the intellectual climate that marked the beginning of the Renaissance, and with this, the rediscovery, editing, distribution, and ultimately printing of the texts of the classical writers which mentioned the Celtic religious orders. We have discussed these texts in the previous chapter, and virtually all became available to scholars by the sixteenth century: very few important sources have come to light since that date with the exception of the Berne *scholia* on Lucan, discovered and published in 1869. Caesar, Pliny, Tacitus and the rest were becoming available in manuscript form from the fifteenth century: Caesar was printed in Venice in 1511, Tacitus in Rome four years later. In England, translations were appearing in quantity by the end of the century. Sir Henry Savile translated part of the *Histories* of Tacitus in 1591, and a second edition seven years later was accompanied by translations of the *Annals* and the *Germania* by Richard Grenewey. Philemon Holland, the 'translator-general', produced lively if free versions of many of the classics, including Pliny's *Natural History* in 1601 and Ammianus Marcellinus in 1609; Clement Edmonds translated Caesar's *Commentaries* in 1604 with his own Observations. The main Druidic references were now widely available not only to scholars reading them in the original, but to the ordinary educated man.

The information was there, but it could not necessarily be set in its appropriate historical framework except in so far as it related to the narrations contained in the Greek and Roman writers. Any recognition of the nature of the Celtic world to which the Druids belonged depended on the concept of a long prehistoric barbarian past upon which, in Western Europe as elsewhere, the classical world impinged. This past was eventually to be elucidated by the as then unapprehended techniques of archaeology, but although these had not been brought into being by the sixteenth century, a pre-classical past of a kind had by no means been ignored. Its existence was of course implicit in the Old Testament narrative, and above all the account of the Deluge, and the subsequent peopling of the world by the progeny of Noah's three sons, Shem, Ham and Japhet. Any reconstruction of the human past had inevitably to start with this indisputable and divinely recorded incident, and a general consensus of opinion had been reached that Europeans were descended from Japhet through his son Gomer. This is not the place to examine the tangled philology that came to be based on the delusive assonances of Gomeri and Cimbri, Cimmerii and Cymry, until Welsh was Hebrew, or Cimbric (ancestral to Saxon) spoken by Adam and Eve, but the mythology of the Sons of Gomer, as we shall see, was to bedevil British antiquity until the nineteenth century. Any consideration of Druids among ancient Gauls or Britons from the Renaissance onwards had for centuries to accommodate them within one or another ancestor-myth that gave Europeans a satisfactorily respectable pedigree back to Noah and the Garden of Eden.

But there were various mythologies current, the most egregious of which was the wholly spurious text and bogus commentary written by Annius of Viterbo, put out in 1498 as a true history of the peopling of the world after the Flood and attributed to a genuine Babylonian historian, Berosus. In this Annius used classical texts relating to Druids, taking from them names and titles, and turning them into fictional kings of the ancient Celts. So we have Dryius, Bardus, Celte and Samothes, the last a misreading of the word *semnotheoi* in Diogenes Laertius which we have encountered in chapter III, and Sarron, who owes his existence to a copyist's error of *sarronidas* for *drovidas* in Diodorus Siculus. In Britain, the twelfth-century fabrication of early British history by Geoffrey of Monmouth maintained its authority into the sixteenth century among the scholastic die-hards, and when the new forgery of Annius was taken up in England by Bale and Caius as late as the 1550's, John White of Basingstoke combined the two mythologies into one compendious, exciting and quite fictitious national pedigree. But by the end of the century the sound scholarship and dispassionate approach to the past of such as William Camden prepared the way for a view of the Druids against a background of fact rather than fiction.

On the Continent the sixteenth century showed a revival of interest in the Druids along rather different lines. Particularly in France, the pre-

LE RE'VEIL
DE L'ANTIQVE
TOMBEAV
DE CHYNDONAX
PRINCE DES VACIES,
DRVIDES, CELTIQVES,
DIIONNOIS.

Auec les Ceremonies des anciennes Sepultures,
briefuement & clairement raportées,

PAR

M. I. GVENEBAVLT Docteur
en Medecine à Dijon.

Dieu fait grace & misericorde à ceux qui la font aux
trespassez, Liure 2. des Roys, chap. 2.

SE VEND A PARIS,
Chez IEAN DAVMALLE, ruë S. Iacques, aux quatre
Elemens, prés le College du Plessis.

M. DCiXXIII.
Auec Priuilege du Roy.

82 Title-page of Guenebault's *Reveil de l'antique Tombeau de Chyndonax*, 1623.

Roman past was seized on as the foundation of a national myth, in which
Gauls or Germans were made into highly respectable ancestors. Justus
Bebelius wrote on the philosophy of the ancient Germans in 1514, and
this was followed by a series of eulogistic accounts of the Gaulish Druids.
Jean le Fèvre in 1532 wrote in French of *Les Fleurs et Antiquitez des Gaules,*
où il est traité des Anciens Philosophes Gaulois appellez Druides; Picard in

ELIÆ SCHEDII
De
DIS GERMANIS,
Sive
Veteri GERMANORVM, GALLO-
RVM, BRITANNORVM, VAN-
DALORVM *Religione*
Syngrammata Quatuor.

Amſterodami,
Apud Ludovicum Elzevirium. Anno 1648.

83 Title-page of Elias Schedius, *De Dis Germanis*, 1648, showing grove, Druid, human sacrifices, drum, skull and cross-bones.

1556 and Forcadel in 1579 associated the Gauls with the Annius mythology and the latter, a lawyer of Toulouse, in his *De Gallio Imperio et Philosophia*, shows a professional interest in the legal powers of the Druids. The title of Noel Taillepied's book of 1585 abundantly describes its scope – *Histoire de l'estat et répub' liques des Druides, Eubages, Sarronides, Bardes, Vacies, anciens François, gouverneurs des pais de la Gaule, depuis le déluge universel, iusques à la venue de Jésus Christ en ce monde. Compris en deux livres, contenans leurs loix, police, ordonnances, tant en l'estat ecclésiastique, que séculier.* Here we have many familiar names – *euhages* and *vates*, Druids and Bards, and Sarronides out of Annius – and the Druidic legal code is set out under the impressive heading of *Ordonnances des Druides Iurisconsultes S.P.Q.G.*, the Senate and People of Gaul, in twenty sonorous sections. Taillepied dated the Flood to 2800 years after the Creation, and so on the accepted chronologies of the day took back Gauls and Druids to about 1200 BC.

81

Much the same theme was pursued on the Continent in the following century. Guenebault in 1623 published a cinerary urn found near Dijon with a suspect inscription in Greek which he read as commemorating one Chyndonax, not only a Druid, but 'Prince de Vacies, Druides, Celtiques, Dijonnois', the last a nice touch of local pride. The Druids as lawgivers continued to receive respectful attention: François Meinhard in 1615 published a Latin oration on The Mistletoe of the Druids as the Symbol of Jurisprudence. Patriotic feeling had demanded Druids among the Germans as well as among the Gauls since the time of Bebelius in 1514, and the sub-title of Elias Schedius' *De Dis Germanis* of 1648 was The Ancient Religion of the Germans, Gauls, Britons and Vandals. Schedius, and Esaias Pufendorf in his *Dissertatio de Druidibus* of 1650, made much of Druidic groves, turf altars and human sacrifices, and the engraved title-page of *De Dis Germanis* shows, in a most unedifying mood of hard primitivism, a grove strewn with decapitated human corpses, and if the robed and oak-wreathed Druid himself looks dignified and venerable enough, he wields a blood-stained sacrificial knife and is attended by a most sinister priestess, slung round with a human skull, and a drum on which she beats with a pair of thigh-bones.

82

83

DRUIDS, ANCIENT BRITONS AND RED INDIANS

We will return to this macabre scene again, for behind it in part must lie an important factor conditioning thought on the ancient inhabitants of Europe from the fifteenth century onwards, the intellectual and emotional impact of the discovery of primitive man in the New World. This is a theme which has been much discussed, and with it must be taken the almost simultaneous confrontation of the Elizabethans with the traditional Irish way of life which had persisted up to the time of the Plantations. It was the American Indian rather than the Irish Celt that influenced concepts of ancient Britons, Germans or Gauls, but although the Elizabethans did not realize that in Ireland they were encountering the Christianized tail-end of the pagan Celtic Iron Age to which the

84 Drawing of American Indian with body-paint, by John White, 1585.

Druids belonged, the recognition of alien Celtic culture within the British Isles, to be reinforced later in the Scottish Highlands, must have made possible a view of the British past hardly hinted at by the Welsh, so long assimilated to English culture.

The American encounters, looked at in the terms already used in the last chapter, produced the reactions of both hard and soft primitivism among Europeans. At first, and throughout in the main, it was hard primitivism that prevailed. From the beginning, the discovery of the aboriginal inhabitants of the Americas raised extremely awkward questions. Some of these were doctrinal, and fundamental – how could these savage heathens be related to the peopling of the world after the Deluge by the progeny of Noah? Were they too to be regarded as automatically damned, or could the inconvenient question be evaded by denying them full human status? Here we immediately recognize the origin of Primitive Man as Caliban, and the less inconvenient but still disturbing possibility began to present itself, that in the strange habits and customs of the American Indians respectable Englishmen might be seeing those of their ancestors the Ancient Britons. On the whole, sixteenth-century antiquaries seemed quite prepared to accept such a view. What was important to Camden, for instance, whose influence was great, was that the Britons, by now coming to be seen linguistically and culturally as part of the ancient European Celtic world, were brought from barbarism to civilization by the beneficent action of the Roman Conquest, and that this was followed by that of the Saxons.

85 Drawings of Ancient
Britons in war-paint by
Lucas de Heere, 1575.

Early commentators on Caesar such as Clement Edmonds in 1604
were not really interested in the Britons; for him the campaign of 56–55
BC 'afoordeth little matter of discourse, being indeed but a scambling
warre'. Philemon Holland, freely translating Pliny in 1601, does not try
to romanticize 'the Druidae (for so they call their Diviners, Wisemen
and the state of their clergy)', concluding his account of the mistletoe
ceremony with the unimpressive version, 'then fall they to kil the beasts
aforesaid for sacrifice, mumbling many oraisons and praying devoutly',
and later summing up, 'so vain and superstitious are many nations of the
world, and oftentimes in such frivolous and foolish things as these'.
Translating as freely as he does, Holland could have easily given the
passages a more favourable tone had he wished to romanticize the
Druids. Samuel Daniel in 1612 explicitly compared the tribal warfare of
the American Indians, in 'the west world lately discovered', with that
likely to have obtained in pre-Roman Britain, and John White, who   84
made brilliant drawings of Virginian Indians when on Raleigh's 1585
expedition, used their distinctive characteristics in portraying Britons
and Picts, and through the engravings of these in de Bry's *America* of
1590 they found their way on to the title-page of John Speed's *Historie*
of Britain in 1611. Indeed, before White, in 1575, the Dutchman Lucas   85
de Heere drew 'les premiers Anglois comme ils alloyent en guerre du
temps du Julius César' as very woe-begone naked savages, and we saw
how Schedius had no reason to play down the barbarity of Druidic
human sacrifice in his title-page of 1648.

A year later John Aubrey wrote a sketch of ancient Wiltshire. He starts with the natural background: 'Let us imagine what kind of a countrie this was in the time of the ancient Britons . . . a shady dismal wood: and the inhabitants almost as savage as the beasts whose skins were their only raiment. The language British. . . .' He goes on to describe their use of coracles, and (like Samuel Daniel) thinks 'that there were several *Reguli* which often made war upon another: and the great ditches which run on the plaines and elsewhere for so many miles (not unlikely) their boundaries'. 'Their religion,' he then says, 'is at large described by Caesar. Their priests were Druids. Some of their temples I pretend to have restored, as Avebury, Stonehenge, &c., as also British sepulchres. Their waie of fighting is lively sett down by Caesar. . . . They knew the use of iron. They were two or three degrees I suppose less savage than the Americans.' What Aubrey has done is to combine the information in Caesar with the reports of the New World voyages in credible and simple form; to this he adds inferences drawn from his archaeological field-work in Wiltshire which were to have unexpectedly far-reaching repercussions on the creation of Druids-as-wished-for which have lasted until today. But the mood is that of hard primitivism, and we are reminded that Aubrey was the friend and biographer of Thomas Hobbes of Malmesbury, the political philosopher who two years later, in his *Leviathan* of 1651, published his famous estimate of primitive peoples, living in 'continuall feare, and danger of violent death; And the life of man, solitary, poore, nasty, brutish and shorte'.

Yet side-by-side with this sombre view of primitive man, prompted by the New World discoveries, there were those who maintained a mood of soft primitivism towards the same phenomena. Pigafetta found virtuous savages on Magellan's voyage of 1511; Peter Martyr wrote in the same year that the New World natives 'seem to live in that golden worlde of whiche the old writers speake so much . . . the golden worlde without toyle', and Arthur Barlowe made his classic statement on the Virginian Indians in 1584. 'Wee found,' he wrote, 'the people most gentle, loving and faithfull, void of all guile, and treason, and such as lived after the manner of the golden age.' Gentle, faithful and guiltless of treason, the American Indian, *dikaiototon anthropon*, takes his place with Homer's Abioi, Strabo's Scythians, or the Druids of Posidonius. Fiction may have fed the fancy in some of the narratives – it has been suggested for instance that de la Vega, in his *History of Peru* of 1617, 'viewed the reality of the Inca Empire . . . through Moore's Utopian eyes' – but at all events the Noble Savage was now in the minds of such as Montaigne, and some of those who wrote on Druids.

Michael Drayton in his *Polyolbion* of 1622 saw the Druids as 'sacred Bards' and philosophers 'like whom great Nature's depths no man yet ever knew', and the young Milton in *Lycidas* (1637) and some of the earlier Latin poems wrote of them in terms of vague but respectful admiration, even if in later life he was to write sourly of the Britons as 'progenitors not to be glori'd in' and of the Druids, 'philosophers I cannot call them, men reported factious and ambitious'. When Druids appeared on the English stage for the first time they did so in a vaguely pastoral and elegiac setting, as bards performing the dignified equivalent of a song-and-dance act in John Fletcher's *Bonduca* of 1618. Boudica, in an alternatively corrupt form of Boadicea, had not yet become a well-known national heroine leading an Ancient British resistance movement; Fletcher took his unfamiliar version of the name from the reading *Boundouka* in the Greek text of Dio. But the anti-Roman Briton or Druid, stoutly defending his island against the foreign invader, was to make a popular appeal a century or so later, enshrined in the poetry of Thomson, Collins, Gray and many others as the outcome of a climate of feeling very different from that of Camden and his contemporaries.

In the meantime, those who wrote on Druids in the later seventeenth and earlier eighteenth centuries usually based their accounts on the main classical references in the Posidonian tradition and did not minimize the barbarity of their human sacrifices. Aylett Sammes in his *Britannia Antiqua Illustrata* (1676) thought Druids supplanted Phoenician 86 bards in Britain – 'it happened that in continuance of time, the DRUIDS got the upper hand' – and instead of dilating on their philosophical attainments makes much of their idolatry and human sacrifices, including the burning of victims alive in the famous basket-work images as described by Caesar, and he adorns this passage with a spirited engraving of the process often to be reproduced by subsequent writers. In the 1720's the Reverend Henry Rowlands, in his *Mona Antiqua Restaurata* of 1723 does not play down Druidic sacrifices nor the hold he thought the priesthood had on 'the abus'd People' by their threats of excommunication or execution, and John Toland in his *History of the Druids* (1726) is highly sarcastic about their skill not only in juggling but in sophistry: he sardonically concedes that 'to be masters of both, and withal to learn the art of managing the mob, which is vulgarly called *leading the people by the nose*, demands abundant study and exercise'. As an amusing parenthesis, we may note that both Rowlands and Toland regarded Abaris the Hyperborean as a Druid, and respectively claim him as a Welshman and as a Highlander. Rowlands thought the name Abaris was corrupted from someone 'sirnamed perhaps ap Rees', while Toland, by translating the Greek *chlamys* as 'plaid', was able to render the description of Abaris in Himerius as 'his body wrapt up in a plad . . . and wearing trowzers reaching from the soles of his feet to his waste', and so triumphantly to present the mythical barbarian sage as dressed 'in the native garb of an aboriginal Scot'. Abaris was fair game for any antiquary of the day: John Wood, the architect of Bath, writing in the 1740's, claimed him as in fact the equally mythical Bladud of Aquae Sulis.

On the whole then the general attitude of scholars and the educated public they addressed on Celts and Druids was, by the early eighteenth century, objective and unromantic. Although the idealizing view of Druid philosophy implicit in the Alexandrian group of sources carried some intermittent weight, the mood was mainly one derived from the Posidonian tradition. On the Continent, idealization was generally

BRITANNIA

ANTIQUA ILLUSTRATA:

OR, THE

ANTIQUITIES

OF ANCIENT

BRITAIN,

Derived from the *Phœnicians* :

Wherein the Original Trade of this ISLAND is difcovered, the Names of
Places, Offices, Dignities, as likewife the Idolatry, Language, and Cuftoms of the Primitive
Inhabitants are clearly demonftrated from that Nation, many old Monuments illuftrated, and
the Commerce with that People, as well as the *Greeks*, plainly fet forth and collected out of
approved Greek and Latin Authors.

TOGETHER

With a CHRONOLOGICAL HISTORY of this Kingdom, from the firft Traditional
Beginning, until the year of our Lord 800, when the Name of BRITAIN was changed into
ENGLAND; Faithfully collected out of the beft Authors, and difpofed in a better Method than hitherto hath been done; with the Antiquities of the *Saxons*, as well as *Phœnicians*, *Greeks*, and *Romans*.

The Firft Volume.

By *AYLETT SAMMES*, of *Chrift*'s Colledge in *Cambridge*.
Since, of the *Inner-Temple*.

——*Si quid Novifti rectius iftis
Candidus imperti, fi non, his utere mecum.* Horatius.

LONDON.
Printed by *Tho. Roycroft*, for the Author, MDCLXXVI.

86 Title-page of Aylett Sammes, *Britannia Antiqua Illustrata*, 1676.

applied to the Druids as law-givers, and for patriotic reasons; the Gauls in particular were moving into that privileged position in early French history favoured by nationalistic sentiment up to this day. In Aubrey's tentative association of Stonehenge and other prehistoric stone circles with the Druids was the germ of an idea which was to run like lunatic wildfire through all popular and much learned thought, and particularly emotive feeling, until modern times, and we will shortly pursue this theme. The discovery of the American Indians played its part in the development of a hard primitivism with regards to Ancient Britons and their religion, but although in fact the Elizabethans had met early Celtic society face-to-face in Ireland, the implications of this for a view of the world of the Druids in pre-Roman Britain or Gaul were not appreciated. Hard primitivism can perhaps be seen as an outcome of a mood of national confidence in the contemporary ethos; the psychological need for a past containing Noble Savages, Golden Ages and primitive un-tutored intimations of immortality as a part of Great Nature's simple plans, seemingly not felt by the Elizabethan and succeeding generations, came perhaps with a changed attitude of personal or social doubt and unease. From the middle of the eighteenth century it seems to have been increasingly felt by many that the rules of taste and the Age of Reason did not provide wholly adequate and inevitably satisfying standards for thought and emotion, and with the distrust of the ultimate validity of the doctrines of the Enlightenment, an alternative mood, emotive and romantic, seemed once more appropriate for the con-templation of the remote past. With this swing of mood, the accommo-dating Druids could change their character and take on a suitably romantic cast of countenance.

THE DRUIDS AND STONEHENGE

With the rediscovery of the Druids in the pages of the Greek and Roman writers came the recognition that they worshipped in forest clearings or groves. The earlier antiquaries, such as Schedius or Pufendorf, assigned them sacrificial altars built of turf and set in appropriately gloomy glades of oak-trees which, on Pliny's authority, sprouted mistletoe. The oaks took on a deeper significance when the Biblical pedigree of the ancient European barbarians was being explored and invented, for could these not be the oaks on the Plain of Mamre recorded in the Old Testa-ment? 'Lo the *Oke Priests!*' exclaimed Edmund Dickinson in 1655, 'Lo the *Patriarchs* of the *Druides!* From these sprang the *Sect* of the *Druides*, which reached up at least, as high as *Abraham's* time,' and this idea was shared by Thomas Smith in his *Syntagma de Druidum moribus ac institutis* of 1644. The Druidic grove, unequivocally described in the classical 87 sources, continued in general favour among antiquaries, artists, poets and the public, into the eighteenth century and beyond. In the eigh-teenth century its popularity was renewed. By the antiquaries, Druids were being transformed into the virtuous sages of ancient Britain, almost indistinguishable from Old Testament patriarchs and prophets, and even sometimes proleptically Christians; among theologians, the deists were discovering that Natural Religion went back to the days of primitive man and was indeed as old as the world; men of sensibility were developing a concept of Nature in her wilder forms as an exemplar, and in such a mood were beginning to appreciate romantic qualities in Gothic architecture. The forest glade, the shaded grove, acquired religious overtones remote from the corpse-strewn *nemeton* thought of by Schedius. William Stukeley in his *Itinerarium Curiosum* of 1724 seems one of the first to derive Gothic architecture from a sylvan prototype – ''tis the best manner of building, because the idea of it is taken from a walk of trees, whose touching heads are curiously imitated by the roof' – and his friend Bishop Warburton later was to link this with the sacred groves of the heathen Goths. 'This northern people,' he wrote, 'having been accustomed, during the gloom of Paganism, to worship the Deity in groves,' it was natural that their first Christian churches should be 'ingeniously projected to resemble groves as nearly as the distance of architecture would admit.' Druids and pagan Gothic priests were inextricably muddled in the minds of many of the time, and what went for one, went for the other. Stukeley, who as we shall see shortly held very different alternative views about Druid temples, still found it fitting in the 1760's to open a very unorthodox doxology at the end of a sermon on Balaam: 'As once in groves, so here in their representative fabrics, we adore the three sacred persons of the deity.' And for those believing in Natural Religion, groves were automatically sacred, and Joseph Warton in 1740 could ask rhetorically why 'mistaken man' should choose

> To dwell in palaces and high-roof'd halls
> Than in God's forests, architect supreme?

Groves, then, were thought by most up to the earlier eighteenth century, and by many later, to be the appropriate temples of the Druids, whether as barbaric priests or as patriarchal philosophers. By a wry twist, it was the beginnings of field archaeology that led to a disastrous change of view. We saw that Aubrey, writing of Druids in prehistoric Wiltshire in 1659, said: 'Some of their Temples I pretend to have restor'd, as Avebury, Stonehenge, &c.' 'Pretend' is of course used here in the sense of 'claim' (as in a Pretender to a throne) and the claim was in fact a perfectly reasonable one in the circumstances. He had used the classical references to pre-Roman Britain sensibly, and to this documentary evidence he added the results of his first-class pioneer field-work at the great henge monuments of Avebury and Stonehenge, and his knowledge that other minor stone circles existed in western Britain. Contrary, as we shall see, to the views of many contemporaries, he did not regard such monuments as of Roman or later date, but as Ancient British, and as in character they could not be interpreted as domestic or defensive structures, nor as primarily sepulchral, he was left with the assumption that they were ceremonial or religious centres, or in other words, unroofed temples. We have not improved on Aubrey's reasoning today,

There, where the spreading consecrated Boughs
Fed the sage Mistletoe, the holy DRUIDS
Lay rapt in moral Musings.— Mason's Elfrida.

These mighty Piles of Magic-planted Rock,
Thus rang'd in mistic order, mark the Place
Where but at times of holiest festival
The DRUID leads his train.— Mason's Caractacus.

87 Druid in a grove with sickle, mistletoe, and Stonehenge, vignette from title-page of Francis Grose, *Antiquities of England and Wales*, 1773–87, vol. IV.

and in the short perspective of prehistory which was then the only one to imagine, he made the monuments contemporary with the classical references to a pre-Roman priesthood, and turned his prehistory into text-aided archaeology by assigning to the Druids his untenanted temples.

He seems to have discussed his ideas with Edward Lhwyd of the Ashmolean, who thought Aubrey's projected account of stone circles 'very well deserves publishing', and who himself wrote to a correspondent of such monuments: 'I conjecture they were Places of Sacrifice and other religious Rites in the Times of Paganism, seeing the *Druids* were our antient heathen Priests.' Aubrey also corresponded with Professor James Garden of Aberdeen in 1693, asking him whether there was evidence for a Druidic origin for the local stone circles; Garden was very attracted by the idea, but with true Scottish caution had to admit that he found 'nothing in the names of the monuments or in the tradition that goes about them, which doth particularly relate to the Druids'. John Toland as a young man talked to Aubrey about Druids and stone circles in 1694, and eagerly accepted his views, which seem to have agreed with

88 Medallion portrait
of William Camden.

his own, and although his projected History of the Druids was never to be
written, the substance of some of it survives in three letters addressed to
his patron Lord Molesworth, published posthumously in 1726. Toland's
extreme unpopularity as a daringly unconventional controversialist
and dangerous free-thinker must have rendered his advocacy of stone
circles as Druid temples of little moment to respectable citizens.

Aubrey developed his theme, modestly and reasonably, in a book
which in its entirety has remained in its unpublished state of chaotic
manuscript until today. Originally the title was to be *Templa Druidum*,
but this became relegated to a chapter-heading in a larger *Monumenta
Britannica*. In 1693 proposals were on foot for publishing, but this came
to nothing; Edmund Gibson printed extracts from the *Templa Druidum*
88 in his 1695 edition of Camden, and Aubrey died two years later. A
transcript of the original manuscript was seen, and notes made from it
by a young antiquary of 30 in 1717, Dr William Stukeley, and he, 25
years or so later was to publish a book on Stonehenge, and another
on Avebury, in which Aubrey's modest suggestion was developed into
a fantastic assertion which caught the changing mood of the time, and
has repercussions to this day. It was Stukeley, theorizing wildly and
unwisely after years of some of the best field-work of his time, and for
generations to come, who first really brought the Druids to Stonehenge
in a manner which captured public sentiment.

The association of the monument and the priesthood has become so
established a piece of English folk-lore that it is too often forgotten that
its origins lie no earlier than the late seventeenth century, and that when
Aubrey's suggestion was printed by Gibson in 1695, it was merely one
among several alternative views about the origins of Stonehenge.
Speculation had begun with Geoffrey of Monmouth in 1136 recording
the legends of its magical transport from Ireland by Merlin, and its
setting up on Salisbury Plain as a memorial to the British nobles killed by
Hengist. The alternative medieval view was that it was a marvel, not to
be explained, and the fourteenth-century author of *De Mirabilibus
Britanniae* made the honest admission that 'at what time this was done,
or by what people, or for what memorial or significance, is unknown'.

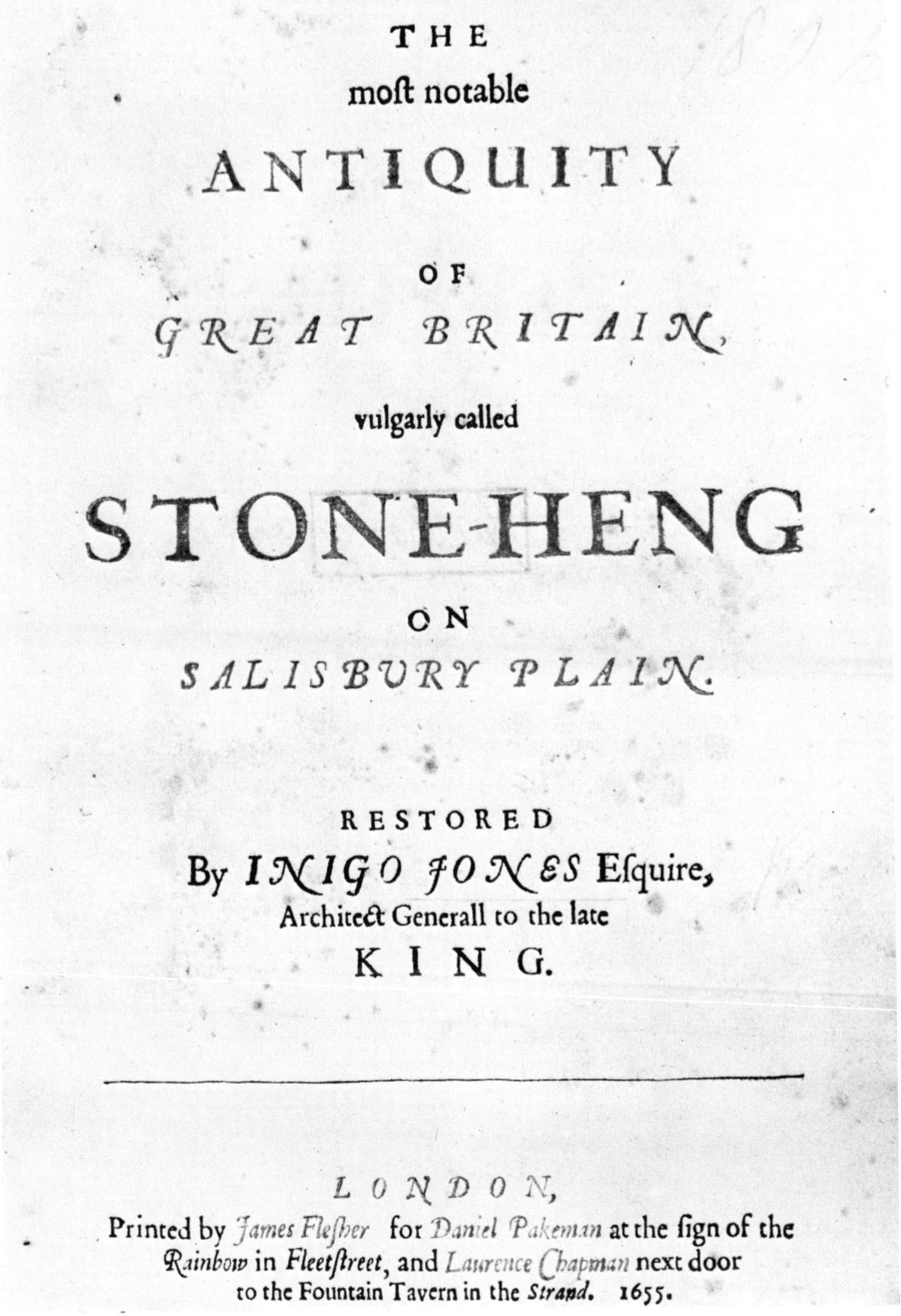

THE
most notable
ANTIQUITY
OF
GREAT BRITAIN,

vulgarly called

STONE-HENG
ON
SALISBURY PLAIN.

RESTORED
By *INIGO JONES* Esquire,
Architect Generall to the late
KING.

LONDON,
Printed by *James Flesher* for *Daniel Pakeman* at the sign of the
Rainbow in *Fleetstreet,* and *Laurence Chapman* next door
to the Fountain Tavern in the *Strand.* 1655.

89 Title-page of Inigo Jones, *Stone-heng*, 1655.

Camden repeated Geoffrey's stories, thought some of the stones artificial, and quoting Cicero called it, unjustifiably, an *insana substructio*, but from the early seventeenth century more positive suggestions were being put forward. Some thought it British: 'that STONAGE is a work of the BRITANNS, the rudenesse it selfe perswades', wrote Edmund Bolton in 1624, who thought it the tomb of Boudica. John Gibbons, in a high-spirited essay, *A Fools Bolt soon Shott at Stonage* in 1666, thought it 'an old British Triumphal Trophical Temple', and Robert Plot in 1686 saw it as 'some British forum or temple'. Aylett Sammes in 1676 had assigned its building to the Phoenicians.

Chronologically, the next school of thought was that which (improbably enough) considered Stonehenge and other stone circles as Roman monuments. Here the earliest and chief protagonist was Inigo Jones, who as the most eminent English architect of his day working in the classical idiom, should have known better than to 'restore', in the words of his title-page, *The most notable Antiquity of Great Britain, vulgarly called Stone-heng* to the Romans in the guise of a temple of the Tuscan order. Jones' book was published posthumously in 1655 by his nephew by marriage, John Webb, and in it he thoroughly discusses the possible claims of Druids and Britons, but dismisses them on the grounds that the classical sources give no indication that they had any architectural competence (which is true enough), and he demolishes Edmund Bolton's ideas about Boudica. Following the criticisms of Charleton and others, Webb re-stated the Roman argument in 1665, and apart from Stonehenge, other stone circles were, by the early eighteenth century, being considered as Roman. Those at Stanton Drew in Somerset, the peculiarly Druidic character of which later antiquaries were to claim on the grounds of the recent place-name, were planned by William Musgrave in his

90 Aerial view of stone circles and alignments, Stanton Drew, Somerset.

91, 92 Illustration of Stonehenge from Walter Charleton, *Chorea Gigantum*, 1663, and title-page of the book.

CHOREA GIGANTUM,

OR,

The moſt Famous Antiquity of

GREAT-BRITAN,

Vulgarly called

STONE-HENG,

Standing on *Salisbury* Plain,

Reſtored to the

DANES;

By *Walter Charleton*, D͡ in Phyſic, and Phyſician
in Ordinary to His Majeſty.

Quæ per conſtructionem lapidum , & marmoreas moles, aut
terrenos tumulos in magnam eductos altitudinem , conſtant ;
non propagabunt longam diem : quippe & ipſa intereunt.

Seneca, de Conſolat. ad Polyb.

LONDON,
Printed for *Henry Herringman* , at the Sign of the *Anchor* in
the Lower Walk of the *New Exchange.* 1663.

Antiquitates Britanno-Belgicae of 1719 without mention of the name of the village, and classified as Roman sepulchral monuments. Avebury was thought to be Roman by Thomas Twining, who wrote on the monument in 1723; Thomas Hearne was also holding this view six years later, and in a poem of 1733 by Samuel Bowden we read how:

> Old *Avebury's* Relicks feed the curious Eye
> And great in Ruins *Roman* structures lie.

91, 92   The third claimants as the builders of Stonehenge were the Danes, particularly championed by Dr Walter Charleton in his *Chorea Gigantum* of 1663. Sir William Dugdale gave his grave approval to the idea, and John Dryden commemorated it in a panegyric poem; Dr Plot was later (1677) to consider that the Rollright stone circle in Oxfordshire might be Danish too, for the name reminded him of Rollo. What influenced Charleton was the publication by the Danish antiquary Ole Worm of descriptions and drawings of Danish megalithic monuments in 1643 and 1651. Unable to accept Inigo Jones' theory of Stonehenge as a Roman temple, he sent a copy of the book to Worm, and in correspondence decided that 'a perfect *Resemblance* in most, if not in all Particulars, observable on both sides' between the 'rudely-magnificent Structures' in Wiltshire and Denmark made it clear that Stonehenge was built by the Danes, 'principally, if not wholly, design'd to be a *Court Royal* or Place for the *Election* and *Inauguration* of their *Kings*'. Charleton, like many an archaeologist since his day, was misled by simple superficial resemblances between monuments built of big stones, and hampered by the absence of any chronology that could separate Worm's prehistoric megalithic tombs from the historical Danes in England in the ninth century A D. The German, Georg Keysler, who travelled extensively in northern Europe and had lived in England, followed a rather similar line in his thoughtful *Antiquitates Selectae Septentrionales et Celticae* of 1720, when he made Stonehenge a Saxon monument because of the occurrence of megalithic chambered tombs in Schleswig-Holstein. With all these conflicting theories circulating among the learned, small wonder that the Druids had no better chance of public sympathy than the rest of the Stonehenge claimants, and the average man must have agreed with Walter Pope, writing *The Salsbury-Ballad* in 1676:

> I will not forget these Stones that are set
> In a round, on *Salsbury* Plains
> Tho' who brought 'em there, 'tis hard to declare,
> The Romans, or Merlin, or Danes.

The idea that Stonehenge (and other stone circles) could have been Druid temples was, as we saw, discussed by John Aubrey and his antiquarian friends in the 1690's, but its publication, in competition with Phoenicians, Romans, Saxons and Danes, had been unfortunate. No more than extracts were printed from Aubrey's volume, and the almost hysterical opposition aroused by any ideas of Toland's would

Mona Antiqua Restaurata.

A N

Archæological Difcourfe

ON THE

ANTIQUITIES,

NATURAL and HISTORICAL,

OF THE

ISLE of *ANGLESEY*,

THE

Antient Seat of the *Britiſh Druids.*

In Two ESSAYS.

With an APPENDIX, containing a Comparative Table of Primitive Words, and the Derivatives of them in feveral of the Tongues of *Europe*; with Remarks upon them.

Together with fome LETTERS, and three CATALOGUES, added thereunto.

I. Of the Members of Parliament from the County of *Angleſey.*
II. Of the High-Sheriffs; And,
III. Of the Beneficed Clergy thereof.

By *HENRY ROWLANDS*, Vicar of *Llanjdan*, in the Iſle of *ANGLESEY*.

DUBLIN:
Printed by AARON RHAMES, for ROBERT OWEN, Bookfeller in *Skinner-Row*,
MDCCXXIII.

93 Title-page of Henry Rowlands, *Mona Antiqua Restaurata*, 1723.

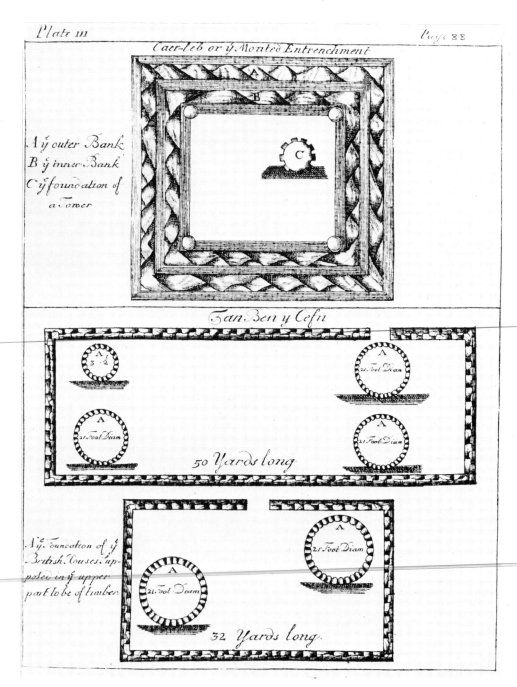

Caer-Leb or ÿ Monted Entrenchment

A ÿ outer Bank
B ÿ inner Bank
C ÿ foundation of
a Tower

Tan Ben y Cefn

A . 1
3 . 2

A
21 Foot Diam

A
21 Foot Diam

A
21 Foot Diam

50 Yards long

A ÿ foundation of ÿ
British Houses sup-
posed in ÿ upper
part to be of timber

A
21 Foot Diam

A
21 Foot Diam

32 Yards long.

94 Illustration showing a rectangular earthwork at Caer Leb, and prehistoric stone hut-circles and enclosures at Tan Ben y Cefn in Anglesey.

142

hinder acceptance of his admittedly quirkily presented case for the Druids in his little essays. Their most persuasive champion was to be William Stukeley in his two publications, on Stonehenge and Avebury, in 1740 and 1743, but the field-work on which these were based was carried out between 1719 and 1724, so that before looking in more detail at Stukeley's later ideas, we must note two figures of this period who are not without importance in the Druid story.

The first is the Reverend Henry Rowlands, an Anglesey vicar whose *Mona Antiqua Restaurata* was published in 1723. The specific description by Tacitus of the Druids in Anglesey naturally made Rowlands look for archaeological remains with which they could be associated, and in fact he makes an early use of the very word in his sub-title, *An Archaeological Discourse on the Antiquities* of his island. His Druids are descended from Noah – 'being so near in descent, to the Fountains of true Religion and Worship, as to have had one of *Noah's* Sons for Grandsire or Great-grandsire, may well be imagin'd, to have carried and conveyed here some of the Rites and Usages of that true Religion, pure and untainted.' But he thinks they worshipped in oak groves as on the Plain of Mamre – 'on these lucent Testimonies of Divine Scriptures, the learned *Dickinson* breaks out' in terms we have already quoted. Their altars are cairns, and especially the cap-stones of the denuded ruins of chambered tombs known as cromlechs, and while there is a stone circle at Bryn-gwyn in his parish, he thinks it only ancillary to a sacred grove. Rowlands therefore has patriarchal, Old Testament, Druids, but leaves them in the groves of the classical writers and cannot conceal the references to their barbarity contained in the narrative of Tacitus. His real contribution to the folk-lore of prehistoric megalithic monuments was to be one of the first to invent Druid Altars of stone.

The second contribution to the myths of Druids and stone circles in the early eighteenth century leads to a most intriguing possibility in English architectural history not hitherto suggested. John Wood, born in Bath in 1704, after precocious architectural experience in Yorkshire and London returned to his native city at the age of 21 with two re-markable and highly original building schemes, which were partly brought into being over the years from 1727 to his death in 1754, when they were carried on by his son, John Wood the younger. The father's description of these schemes was not published until 1742, two years after he had made an original and accurate survey of Stonehenge, and drafted an account of the monument ultimately published in 1747. By 1740 he was clearly obsessed by Druids. To them he attributed a Metro-politan Seat in Bath itself, where they worshipped Apollo; a University at the Stanton Drew circles; and four constituent Colleges on Exmoor and Mendip, and at Stonehenge and Avebury: we have already seen that he thought Bladud of Bath was really Abaris the Hyperborean. His projected new buildings in Bath were, in 1725, to include an Imperial Gymnasium, a Royal Forum, and 'another Place, no less magnificent, for the Exhibition of Sports, to be called the *Grand Circus*'. As Sir John Summerson has asked, 'What induced this obviously practical and

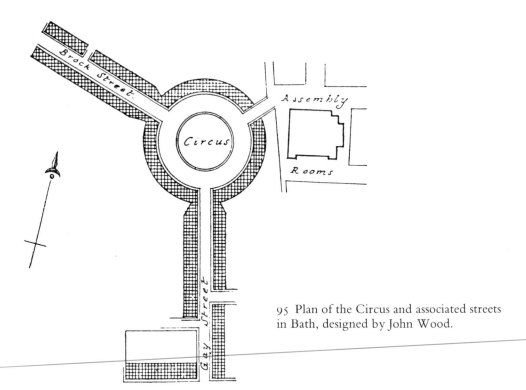

95 Plan of the Circus and associated streets in Bath, designed by John Wood.

competent young builder to put forward this trinity of impossibles?'
The answer, he thought, must surely somehow lie in the architect's
romantic archaeology, 'the catalytic agent which released John Wood's
imaginative power. Every scheme he proposed is coloured by the feeling
that he is restoring antique grandeur.' Architecturally, the Circus at
Bath is one of the most original concepts in European town-planning;
wholly without precedent when designed by Wood, it is 'the pioneer
of all circuses, from Bath to Piccadilly, from Exeter to Edinburgh'. But
why did Wood build it as he did, and what lay behind the concept?
Contemporary men of taste saw part of the answer: 'it looks like
Vespasian's amphitheatre turned outside in', wrote Smollett, and if
Wood, as is quite possible, knew the Colosseum in Rome only from
inadquate little engravings he could have thought it both circular and
small, and designed his unique town block accordingly. But the
Colosseum may not be the whole answer.

There seems to be the exciting possibility that the Circus owes something to the Druids as well. The ideas about Bladud and Stanton Drew
and Stonehenge, Wood wrote down around 1740 must have been in his
mind when he was making his building plans from 1725 onwards, and
indeed he specifically relates the two aspects in his *Essay towards a
Description of Bath* of 1742. The Circus is planned as a true circle about
300 feet in diameter, with three symmetrically spaced entrances: an
unusual lay-out with no prototype in the Colosseum or in classical
architecture at large. Now the only plan of the whole monument of
Stonehenge readily available in the early 1720's was that of Inigo Jones,
in his book of 1655 or its reprint (with Webb and Charleton) published

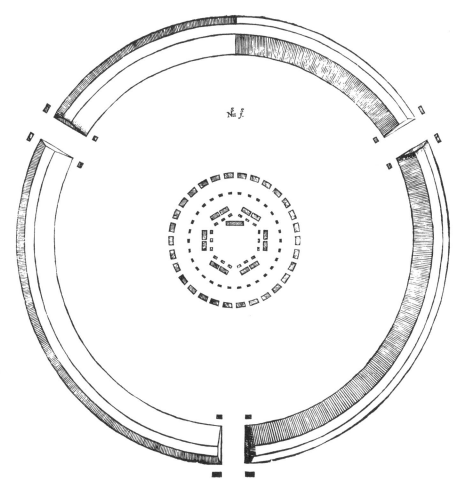

96 Plan of Stonehenge showing three entrances to the bank and ditch, by Inigo Jones, 1655.

in the critical year of Wood's design, 1725, and here the earthwork enclosure of the monument is shown as a boldly drawn geometrical circle some 300 feet in diameter, with three symmetrical gaps which Jones believed it to have originally possessed. As an architect, Wood would have turned to Jones with respect, whatever he thought of Stonehenge as a Temple of the Tuscan Order, and what better than to include elements of a College of the Druids in his Grand Circus to be built in their Metropolitan Seat?

A 'circus' did not necessarily mean a Roman structure at this time, for a circular track for ladies' carriage-exercise was known to Pope as 'Hide-Park Circus' in 1712; 'cirque' was used for 'circle' in seventeenth-century English, and Charleton uses it both for a stone circle described by Ole Worm, and for the Circus Maximus in Rome – 'the great *Cirque*, or the other monstrous Buildings of the *Romans* in *Italy*'. Such classical terms were used without precision, for after all Plot in 1686 had called Stonehenge a 'forum'. And it seems that in the later

97, 98 Obverse and reverse of bronze medallion commemorating William
Stukeley (1687–1765).

eighteenth century someone thought of Avebury as a Druid Circus, for
the cryptic entry on Andrews' and Dury's map of Wiltshire of 1773
against the site, *a Samons Cirens Supposed by Antiquarians to be a Druid
Temple*, must result from a mis-engraving in italic script of an original
Famous Circus. In Wood's delightfully confused archaeological enthusiasm, Druids, Stonehenge, the Circus Maximus and the Colosseum
could well be blended to produce the exquisite architectural conceit with
which he honoured the past of his beloved city.

FROM WILLIAM STUKELEY
TO THE SOUTH SEA ISLANDERS

97, 98   William Stukeley, a young Lincolnshire doctor already with pronounced antiquarian interests, was at the age of 29 attracted to Stonehenge by seeing engravings of the monument made by David Loggan
in the later seventeenth century; three years later, in 1719, he first visited
the site. In the meantime, he had also seen and made notes from a
transcript of Aubrey's *Monumenta*, and by this was led in the same year
to visit the then almost unknown monument of Avebury. From that
time until 1724 he made annual visits to Wiltshire and carried out a
remarkable programme of field-work at both sites, and while at
Avebury in 1723 he began to write a book which was in fact to be his
own version of a *Templa Druidum*, under the original title of *The History
of the Temples of the Ancient Celts*. The use of the word 'Celt' as an alternative to 'Briton' was now coming into general use among British
antiquaries, largely owing to the influence of a book by the Frenchman,
Paul-Yves Pezron, in its English translation by David Jones, *The
Antiquities of Nations, More Particularly of the* Celtae *or* Gauls, *Taken to be
Originally the same People as our* Ancient Britains (1706), in which the
descent of the Celts through Gomer, and so Japhet and Noah, is firmly
set out.

    Stukeley's original book got no further than a manuscript draft, and
99 by 1724 he was thinking of making it a *History of the Ancient Celts* in

O qui me gelidis in vallib'Hæmi
Sistatq; ingenti ramorum protegat umbra:
Fœlix qui potuit Rerum cognoscere causas:

Atq₃ metus Omnes & inexorabile Fatum
Subjecit pedibus, strepitumq; Acherontis
avari. Virg.

THE HISTORY OF
THE TEMPLES
OF THE ANTIENT
CELTS.

99 Pen and wash drawing for the title-page of William Stukeley's projected
book, *The History of the Temples of the Ancient Celts*, July 1723. No Druids are
mentioned and the scene is among rocks and woods.

The history of the Temples & religion of the Druids.

The history of the religion and temples of the DRUIDS.

100 Revised drawing of Stukeley's title-page, with Druids replacing Celts, drawn between 1723 and 1733.

four parts; by 1733 he had drawn a new frontispiece with an amended
100 title, *The History of the Religion and Temples of the DRUIDS*. He had
entered Holy Orders in 1729, and continued his antiquarian pursuits un-
abated, but the publication of his surveys and surmises was delayed until
102 1740, when *Stonehenge, a Temple restor'd to the British Druids* appeared,
101 followed in 1743 by *Abury, a Temple of the British Druids, with Some
Others, Described*. These were announced as two parts only of a work on
Patriarchal Christianity in seven sections, but no more of this *magnum
opus* was to be published. It was intended, in his own words, 'to combat
the deists from an unexpected quarter, and to preserve so noble a monu-

101, 102 Engravings of drawings by William Stukeley of the South Inner Circle at Avebury and of Stonehenge looking east. The Avebury drawing (*above*) was made in 1723 and published in 1743, that of Stonehenge (*below*) in 1722 and published in 1740.

ment [Avebury] of our ancestors' piety, I may add, orthodoxy'. Stonehenge, Avebury and the Druids were in fact presented to the public as part of a complicated religious tract no less than as a record of the monuments themselves. 'My intent is,' he wrote, '(besides preserving the memory of these extraordinary monuments, now in great danger of ruin), to promote, as much as I am able, the knowledge and practice of ancient and true Religion, to revive in the minds of the learned the spirit of Christianity . . . to warm our hearts into that true sense of Religion, which keeps the medium between ignorant superstition and learned free-thinking, between enthusiasm and the rational worship of God, which is no where upon earth done, in my judgement, better than in the Church of *England*.' Since, then, we have to consider Druids-as-wished-for by an eighteenth-century clergyman engaged in religious controversy, we must glance at the controversy itself.

The theological disputes of the seventeenth century had made Christianity the subject of open discussion among the reformed churches, and after the excesses of uncontrolled personal interpretation of the Scriptures and the hair-splitting of the jarring sects, there was a general desire to find some acceptable scheme of religion in which all could find common ground, firmly based on reasoned argument, and 'not to be destroyed or altered by every whiffling Proclamation of an Enthusiast'. With this went the discoveries of the scientists, especially mathematicians like the devout Newton, who had found an ordered universe which could only be the expression of Nature's Law, and ordained by God: as Willey put it, outlining this situation, 'the Great Machine presupposed the Divine Mechanic'. The result, set out by those who professed and called themselves Deists, was a theory of Natural Religion, 'la religion d'Adam, de Seth, de Noe . . . aussi ancienne que le monde', as Voltaire put it in 1752, and this obviously carried with it implications for primitive man, whether in the remote past or surviving to the present day, for all would share in the same faith.

> Nor think in Nature's state they blindly trod;
> The State of Nature was the reign of God

wrote Pope in 1733, and about the same time Haller, a Swiss poet, pointed out that Hurons and Hottentots share a universal duty under Natural Law. The Ancient Britons (and by implication, Druids) would also come within the fold, and Henry Brooke said so in his *Gustavus Vasa* of 1739:

> Great Nature's law, the law within the breast,
> Formed by no art, and to no sect confined,
> But stamped by Heaven upon th'unlettered mind.
> Such, such of old the first born natives were
> Who breathed the virtues of Britannia's air,
> Their realm when mighty Caesar vainly sought
> For mightier freedom against Caesar fought,
> And rudely drove the famed invader home,
> To tyrranize o'er polished – venal – Rome.

Here we have the virtuous British, fired by Natural Religion to shake off the conqueror's threatened yoke in a resistance movement led by the Druids who appear in the apostrophes to Liberty by Thomson in 1735 or Collins in 1747, where the anti-Roman British chiefs:

> Hear their consorted *Druids* sing
> Their Triumphs to th'immortal String,

and we are rapidly approaching Cowper's Boadicea and the Sage beneath a spreading Oak (1782).

But while Natural Religion could create a propitious climate of opinion for virtuous and philosophical Druids, it also raised problems of orthodoxy. Its exponents were Deists and free-thinkers like John Toland, who wrote *Christianity not Mysterious*, and who belittled or repudiated the miraculous elements in the Faith, and undermined the necessity of Revelation. The Deists had found 'all-sufficient evidence of God's existence and of its moral government in "Nature" and in the conscience of man', as Willey put it. 'The natural evidences for the Divine Original were . . . felt to be overwhelming; it was "Revelation" that had to be substantiated.' One way of doing this was to take not only Natural but the Christian religion back to the beginning of time, as the compendious title of Matthew Tindal's book of 1730 announces – *Christianity as Old as the Creation, or the Gospel a Republication of the Religion of Nature*. This was more or less the line taken by Stukeley. His Druids came to England with the Phoenicians (who themselves had first been brought here by Sammes in 1676), 'soon after Noah's flood' and 'during the life of Abraham, or very soon after'. They were 'of *Abraham's* religion intirely' and although 'we cannot say that Jehovah appeared personally to them', they had arrived at 'a knowledge of the plurality of persons in the Deity' so that their religion 'is so extremely like Christianity, that in effect it differ'd from it only in this; they believed in a Messiah who was to come, as we believe in him that is come.' 'I have not scrupled to introduce Druids before a Christian audience,' he later wrote in a preface to some very eccentric sermons, 'they were of the patriarchal religion of ABRAHAM' and 'Christianity is a republication of the patriarchal religion.' The phrase is that of Tindal, whose book, published in his first year in Orders, may well have influenced Stukeley's thinking; certainly, his readers would have seen the connection.

While Stukeley's Patriarchal Religion was for a time forgotten, his advocacy for a Druidic origin for Avebury, Stonehenge and other stone circles long continued to consolidate and reinforce what was now an established piece of national folk-lore. He did not think the idea of Druids sacrificing on the cap-stones of denuded megalithic tombs a happy one, and in an unpublished note sensibly wrote, of Druids and their alleged altars, 'we have no way to separate them but in thinking some of them are too high, & it would be absurd to imagine the priest climbd a ladder to doe his office before the people because it would be highly indecent & abate much of the reverence.' But his Druids were firmly entrenched at Stonehenge, and whatever one might think of the

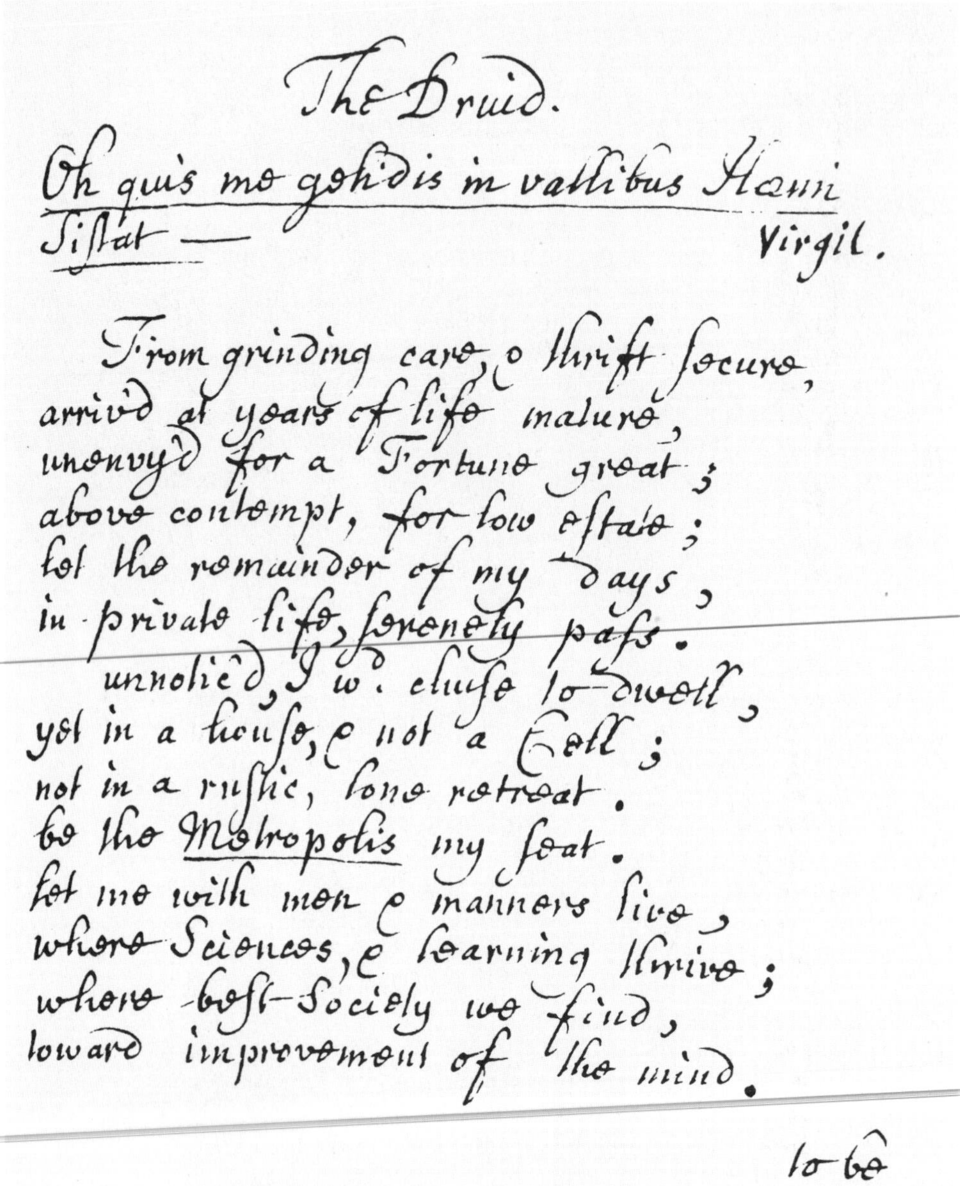

The Druid.

Oh quis me gelidis in vallibus Hæmi
Sistat —   Virgil.

From grinding care, o thrift secure,
arriv'd at years of life mature,
unenvy'd for a Fortune great;
above contempt, for low estate;
let the remainder of my days,
in private life, serenely pass.
      unnotic'd, I w.ᵈ chuse to dwell,
yet in a house, e not a Cell;
not in a rustic, lone retreat.
be the Metropolis my seat.
let me with men e manners live,
where Sciences, e learning thrive;
where best-Society we find,
toward improvement of the mind.

to be

103 'The Druid': opening of autograph of unpublished poem by William
Stukeley, 1758.

103   Archdruid's suitability for a seat on the Bench of Bishops even in a very
Latitudinarian eighteenth-century Church of England, there was no
doubt but that he was a scholar and a gentleman. He and his clergy were
in fact Noble Savages, and by the second half of the eighteenth century
these were exactly what some men of feeling and sensibility were prepared to find among their British ancestors, because they were finding
them elsewhere.

104 Plaque erected by the East India Company commemorating Prince Lee Boo, Rotherhithe Church, London.

The American Indians were now in part being thought of in a sympathetic mood of soft primitivism. Already by the 1770's the Noble Savage speech of the Indian chief Logan, to be recorded by Thomas Jefferson in his *Notes on Virginia* of 1784, was in vogue as a recitation piece for American schoolboys; it is thoroughly in the mood of the fictitious speeches classical writers attributed to Boudica, Calgacus, Vercingetorix or the Scythian philosopher who addressed Alexander. The Scythians, as it happens, were being admired even in the later seventeenth century, when Benjamin Whichcote exclaimed that it was 'a thing to be admired, that *nature* should bestow that on the *Scythians*, which the *Grecians*, long instructed by precepts of philosophers, had not attained! that formed manners should be transcended by uneducated barbarity.' A very close kinship to the speech of Calgacus is seen in that attributed by Samuel Johnson to a 'petty chief' among the Indians of Quebec, who 'from behind the shelter of the bushes contemplated the art and regularity of *European* war', in an *Idler* paper of 1759, and the similarity may well have been intended. But no better speech of this genre can be found than that put into the mouth of Abba Thule, 'King of the Pelew Islands', by George Keate in his charming and exciting account of the discovery of these islands (the Palaus, in the extreme west of the Caroline Islands) in 1788. Abba Thule, and his son Lee Boo who was brought to England and died young in this country, thrilled Men of Feeling of the time:

> Stop, Reader, stop! let NATURE claim a Tear
> A Prince of Mine, LEE BOO, lies bury'd here

says his tombstone. The South Sea Islanders had been discovered, and found to be Children of Nature.

104

From de Brosses in the *Histoire des Navigations* of 1756 to Wilson's account of the missionary activities among the Polynesians in 1799, a whole series of books of travel in the South Seas were published, including not only the famous names such as de Bougainville and Cook, but many lesser writers such as George Keate, already quoted. As a whole, they presented to a public already receptive a picture of an idyllic land inhabited by Noble Savages who could of course be brought conveniently, as Haller brought Hurons and Hottentots, within the fold of Natural Religion and Nature's simple plan, and so create a myth which was to be potent to the time of Gauguin and beyond. In accepting the idealized view, the public too often forgot other aspects of the culture-pattern recorded by the travellers, such as the ruthless power of the Tahitian priests, the *arioi*; their sex life and the resultant infanticide; the human sacrifices and the internecine wars. But perhaps some remembered this, for we find an Oxford Prize Poem *The Aboriginal Britons*, by George Richards (1791), opening, in the words of the Argument, with 'An Address to the first Navigators of the South-Seas':

> Ye sons of Albion, who with venturous sails
> In unknown oceans caught Antarctic gales

and who had:

> View'd on the coast the wondering Savage stand
> Uncouth, and fresh from his Creator's hand;
> While woods and tangling brakes, where wild he ran,
> Bore a rough semblance of primeval man –
> A form like this, illustrious souls, of yore
> Your own Britannia's sea-girt island wore . . .
> Rude as the wilds around his sylvan home,
> In savage grandeur see the Briton roam;
> Bare were his limbs, and strung with toil and cold
> By untam'd nature cast in giant mould.

The mood is hard primitivism, even if 'Britannia's sons' fight stoutly against the Romans, and the Druids are grim figures of dread, worshipping in a grove, striking terror into the enemy's heart by their horrid rites:

> The Roman check'd awhile his conquering hand
> And dropt the imperial Eagle from his hand –

and overawing their own people:

> By rites thus dread the Druid Priests impress'd
> A sacred horror on the savage breast.

By contrast the Bards ('heav'n-born seers, whose magic fingers strung The Cambrian lyre') are noble and inspired apostles of freedom, and perhaps George Richards thought himself a Bard as he declaimed his composition in the Sheldonian Theatre. A year later, at all events, he published *Songs of the Aboriginal Bards of Britain*, somewhat in the manner of Gray's *Bard* of 1758.

By now too the Druids and the South Sea Islanders were together claiming attention in Scotland. It is interesting to notice that James Macpherson does not use Druids as romantic stage properties in his Ossian fabrications such as *Fingal* (1762), though he discusses them at length in his *History of Great Britain* in 1773, but they were so used by John Smith in his similarly invented poems printed in *Galic Antiquities* (1780). In 1787 the Reverend Dr John Ogilvie, minister of Midmar in Aberdeenshire, 'having seen a small Druidical Fane', which must have been one of the local stone circles about which Aubrey and Garden had corresponded, published anonymously a poem, *The Fane of the Druids*, in which he 'endeavoured both to enumerate the institutions of the Druids, and to lay down their principles', hoping that 'the circumstances shall in themselves be interesting to a reader of sensibility'. The Druid Chief is an impressive figure:

> Though time with silver locks adorn'd his head
> Erect his gesture yet, and firm his tread . . .
> His seemly beard, to grace his form bestow'd
> Descending decent, on his bosom flow'd;
> His robe of purest white, though rudely join'd
> Yet showed an emblem of the purest mind.

He bids 'th'assembled tribes' to build a Fane, and a stone circle is built round a central oak-tree at which Pliny's mistletoe ceremony is duly enacted. Other dignified rites take place, in which virgins including the beautiful Florella participate, and her hand is later won by the young warror Edgar. The scene closes in pastoral tranquillity, and the poet asks:

> Ye days of quiet, now beheld no more!
> Where are ye fled? To what far-distant shore?

and where too, he asks, is the Goddess of that simple life, driven away by the madding crowd of modern pleasure-seekers, who even ('Ye bold Aeronauts!') pursue her in balloons?

> Ah! In the depth of Tahaiteean groves
> She dwells with swains that gain unenvied loves! . . .
> Or joins in social isles the mirthful band
> Or leads the dance on Monootopa's strand.
> There sits the Power, from busier scenes convey'd
> There WALKS with NATURE o'er th'unbounded shade;
> There sooth'd to rest, and pleas'd with artless strains,
> Restores a golden age on Indian plains.

From Midmar to Monootopa's strand, from the groves of the Druids to those of a Tahaiteean Golden Age, was no difficult transition for the reader of sensibility in 1787. In Scotland particularly, the State of Nature was being much discussed. Montesquieu's *Esprit des Lois* (1748) and Rousseau's famous *Discours sur l'Inégalité* of 1753 had started the thinking which led to the work of the Scottish Primitivists such as Monboddo, Blackwell and Kames in the 1770's and 1780's, all of them discussing,

105 Illustration of the Carnac alignments from La Tour-d'Auvergne, *Origines Gauloises*, 1796.

in the words of Mr McQueedy, Peacock's comic Scot of a generation later, 'the infancy of society'.

In France, Gaulish Druids were being invented along much the same lines as their British counterparts. We have noticed Pezron's *L'Antiquité de la Nation et la Langue des Celts* of 1703, and already by 1727 Jean Martin has Patriarchal Druids, and may have been influenced by Rowlands, in his *Religion des Gaulois*. Simon Pelloutier's *Histoire des Celtes* was first published in 1740 and was widely influential, going into a second edition in 1770: he sought to equate the Celtic and Teutonic religions for political purposes. The Comte de Caylus included Gaulish antiquities in his great *Recueil des Antiquités*, published between 1752 and 1766, together with Egyptian, Greek, Roman and Etruscan, and seems to have recognized that megalithic monuments might be pre-Druid, but by the end of the century they were firmly Druidic. La Tour-d'Auvergne, in his *Origines Gauloises* of 1796, believed he had found a Breton word 'dolmin' used for a megalithic tomb, and in the form 'dolmen' this entered archaeological jargon. Stone circles being small, rare and inconspicuous in France, they did not play the same part in the Druid myth as did those of Britain, but chambered tombs as dolmens, and alignments of standing stones, especially those of Brittany, were obvious candidates.

Interesting light on the difference between the British and the French approach is provided by the Abbé de Tressan, who had written a book on classical mythology which appeared in an English translation by H. North in 1806. For this edition of his *History of the Heathen Mythology*

105

106 The Heroic Gaul: a late nineteenth-century statue of Ambiorix, chief of the Eburones, at Tongres, Belgium.

107 The Unheroic Druid:
the Druid Panoramix from
the modern French comic
strip series by Goscinny and
Uderzo, *Astérix le Gaulois*.

the Abbé added 'An Enquiry into the Religion of the First Inhabitants of
Britain, And a Particular Account of the Ancient Druids.' In this,
although Mr Macpherson and 'the poetry of the celebrated Ossian' receive
respectful mention, there is no mention of Stonehenge or any temples
other than groves, and the picture painted is essentially a Gaulish one,
with philosophical high-lights and Ossianic shadows, and the usual
confusion with words like Sarronides and Eubages.

Jacques Cambry in his *Monumens Celtiques* (1805) described Breton
megalithic monuments as both Druidic and astronomical in significance,
and by now we are deep in Celtomania. The scene was wittily summed
up by Salomon Reinach; *les celtomanes*, by the nineteenth century,
firmly believed that 'the Celts are the oldest people in the world; their
language is preserved practically intact in Bas-Breton; they were profound philosophers whose inspired doctrines have been handed down
by the Welsh Bardic Schools; dolmens are their altars where their priests
the Druids offered human sacrifice; stone alignments were their astronomical observatories.' As in the sixteenth and seventeenth centuries,
the Druids and the Gauls were far more part of a patriotic myth for
Frenchmen than ever were Druids and Britons for the English; a myth
which in its final form has become the subject for superb slap-stick
ridicule in the *Astérix* comic strips of today. Druids could crop up in the
most extraordinary contexts in nineteenth-century France, and one is
hardly surprised that in the 1860's the enterprising and prolific literary
forger Vrain Lucas not only fabricated letters from Gaulish chieftains,
but one from Lazarus to St Peter in which Druids are discussed.

106

107

By the second half of the eighteenth century in Britain we have, as we have seen, Druids well established in more than one role. According to taste, one could see them as Patriarchal pre-Christian Christians; savages reflecting either the good or the bad qualities of Polynesians real or imagined; worshipping in stone circles (especially Stonehenge) or in groves; sacrificing on the top of megalithic tombs or at a mistletoe-decked oak; encouraging bards or being bards themselves; as fierce anti-Roman champions of liberty as in Mason's play *Caractacus* (1759) or as the colourless and rather gentlemanly priests envisaged by Pope in his projected *Brutus* (1744). But among all these Druids-as-wished-for we have not yet considered an aspect which was to be of increasing significance as the nineteenth century wore on, the Druid as the repository of mystic wisdom or as a Priest of the Ancient Mysteries. It is here that Reinach's reference to doctrines believed to be handed down by bardic schools in Wales is significant.

THE GORSEDD OF THE BARDS OF BRITAIN

The *Gentleman's Magazine* for October 1792 recorded a singular event which had taken place on September 23. 'This being the day on which the autumnal equinox occurred, some Welsh Bards, resident in London, assembled in congress on Primrose Hill, according to ancient usage. . . . The wonted ceremonies were observed. A circle of stones formed, in the middle of which was the *Maen Gorsedd*, or Altar, on which a naked sword being placed, all the Bards assisted to sheath it.' What were these bards doing, making a stone circle, and how ancient was the usage? In answering these questions we find a nice mixture of fact, fantasy and, alas! forgery.

The Welsh bards, even if somewhat fallen on evil days by 1792, were not nonsense. In the Middle Ages, as with their counterparts in Ireland, they had formed part of the traditional Celtic hierarchy with genuine roots in the ancient past of the Celts and Druids. Traditional formulaic composition and complex metrical forms were preserved, cultivated and transmitted by poets, singers and harpists in Wales, and however tenuous, the links of this tradition in the eighteenth century with that of the Middle Ages were genuine enough. From at least the twelfth century there had been in existence an organization or 'court' for regulating and licensing accredited performers in poetry and music, and maintaining standards by competitions and awards, known as an *Eisteddfod*, a session or assembly. In the sixteenth century, *eisteddfodau* at Caerwys were organized partly to limit the number of vagrant bards: the English government, already preoccupied with the problem of 'sturdy beggars', was concerned in Wales as in Ireland with controlling the movements of dangerously mobile elements in Celtic society. The tradition of holding an Eisteddfod intermittently in one or other Welsh town continued feebly until the exceptionally well organized meeting at Corwen in 1789, which gave the institution a vitality and a stability it maintained into the nineteenth century and beyond. But in all the

Welsh meetings there had been no question of a stone circle or a Maen Gorsedd.

It is here that we turn to fancy and fabrication. A Glamorganshire stone-mason, Edward Williams, born in 1747, had been working in London from the early 1770's and was an active member of a group of Welshmen there who were interesting themselves in their national culture, language, literature and antiquities. Williams had been brought up in the poetic and musical conventions current among the traditional poets of Glamorganshire, and according to custom had adopted a 'bardic' nom-de-plume, that of Iolo Morganwg, Iolo of Glamorgan, the name by which he is best known, and in his misguided enthusiasm and local patriotism declared that the Glamorganshire bards had preserved, virtually intact, a continuous tradition of lore and wisdom going back to the original prehistoric Druids. But he did not leave his assertions unsupported. With the prevailing low standards of scholarship in early Welsh linguistics and palaeography it was unfortunately not difficult for Iolo to forge documents to prove his case, and these were in fact a part only of his large corpus of fabrications of early Welsh literature which was to cause so much confusion when more exact scholarship came to be applied to the texts. The Primrose Hill ceremony was another outcome of Iolo's crazy enthusiasm; the quaint little ritual in fact aroused no interest, partly owing to the fact that Iolo's group of associates held views notoriously sympathetic to Tom Paine and the French Revolution. Incidentally, in view of subsequent events, there is no reason to think of the 'circle of stones' reported in the *Gentleman's Magazine* as being anything much more than a ring of pebbles.

We might not have heard of the Gorsedd again had not Iolo seen an opportunity for furthering his nonsense – for it can be called nothing else – by getting it attached to the genuine if moribund Eisteddfod. At the end of the three-day session held at Carmarthen in 1819 the Gorsedd Circle, made of stones taken by Iolo from his pockets, was first set up in Wales, in the garden of the Ivy Bush Hotel, and the bardic performance took place. The Gorsedd, which Iolo originally had hoped might supersede the Eisteddfod, was now assured of a future as an integral part of it, nicely calculated to appeal to nationalists and romantics, the credulous and the pompous. The Gorsedd itself, the Druids, the Ceremony, the Prayer, the Invocation to Peace, the Symbol of the Ineffable Name and the Traditional Rites are traditional only so far as they preserve the romantic imaginings of a somewhat less than honest journeyman mason 160 years ago. As Professor Gwyn Williams has written, 'the inventions of Iolo Morganwg in the eighteenth century and, as a result, the dignified nonsense of the Gorsedd ceremony associated annually with the National Eisteddfod has helped to throw a mist of unreliable antiquarianism about the subject which scholarship has not the means completely to dispel.'

The 'dignified nonsense' of the Gorsedd was not always so dignified in its earlier days. In 1855 a distinguished English poet and man of letters was on a family holiday in Llandudno, and his small sons were excited by a 'large tent-like wooden structure' which they hopefully took to be

108 The Archdruid of the Welsh Eisteddfod.

a circus. It was however the Eisteddfod pavilion. 'My little boys were disappointed,' Matthew Arnold told his Oxford audience two years later in his first Lecture on Celtic Poetry, 'but I, whose circus days are over . . . was delighted.' It was on a day of 'storms of wind, clouds of dust, an angry, dirty sea' that 'the Gorsedd was held in the open air, at the windy corner of a street. . . . The presiding genius of the mystic circle, in our hideous nineteenth century costume relieved only by a green scarf, the wind drowning his voice and the dust powdering his whiskers, looked thoroughly wretched; so did the aspirants for bardic honours.' Today, even if the weather may be no better, the stage properties of high Victoriana enhance the performance: robes by Sir Hubert Herkomer *108* RA and regalia by Sir Goscombe John.

At this point we may appropriately glance at the changing fashions in Druidic costume and accessories. There are of course no ancient representations of Druids, so imagination has had free rein. Earlier representations tended to show them in vaguely classical robes, but the sandalled and bearded figure in Schedius' title-page of 1648 wears a long gown over which is a knee-length tunic with a fringed border, voluminous sleeves and a frilly neck, girded round with a sash; he has an oak-leaf wreath on his head. Keysler in 1720, conflating Celtic and Nordic myth, has a barefoot priest with oak wreath and long belted gown, who is a sort of Druid, while in Britain an interesting series of related types can be seen. These begin with Sammes (1676), whose Druid is barefoot, with a knee-length tunic and hooded cloak, and holds a book in one hand and a staff in the other, and a bag or scrip hangs from his side. He wears no wreath, but has an excessively venerable beard nearly as long as his tunic. Rowlands in 1723 copied this figure, adding sandals and replacing 109 the book with an oak branch, and labelled it 'The Chief Druid'. Stukeley in the same year further modified the Sammes-Rowlands type, considerably shortening the beard of his British Druid, removing the oak branch, turning the scrip into an odd sort of bottle, and hanging a Bronze Age axe-head from the belt. Later in the century some Druids show renewed classical influence, and the Druid statue of 1763 at the entrance to Penicuik House, Midlothian, designed by its owner, Sir James Clerk, whose father, Sir John, was a noted antiquary, is a version of the well-known statue of a barbarian in the Lateran, itself copied by William Kent in his staircase paintings at Kensington Palace in 1724.

But by the time of the Victorian Gorsedd, the main influence at work was that provided by the delightful coloured aquatints in Samuel Rush Meyrick's and Charles Hamilton Smith's *Costume of the Original Inhabitants of the British Islands* (1815), Plate X of which depicts 'An Arch Druid in His Judicial Habit'. The awesome figure, wreathed in oak-leaves, has a full but neat white beard, and a very voluminous white robe. He wears an Early Bronze Age gold lunula upside-down on his head as a diadem, and a Late Bronze Age Irish gold gorget round his neck; a version of this forms part of the modern regalia under the name of *Dwyfronneg yr Archdderwydd*, the Archdruid's Breastplate. The Archdruid in Meyrick and Smith incidentally holds an inscribed wooden grid, the *Coelbren y Beirdd* invented by Iolo. The rest of the Gorsedd regalia, the Sceptre, the Sword, the Crown and the Hirlas Horn, have no antecedents beyond the romantic invention and singularly bad taste of their designer.

THE DRUIDS AND THE MYSTICS

The influence of Iolo was not confined to the invention of the Gorsedd, for his Druidic fabrications were to poison the wells of genuine scholarship in early Celtic literature for generations to come. In the second half of the eighteenth century serious attempts were being made to collect, examine and translate early Celtic poetry, particularly that of Wales. The appearance of Macpherson's Ossianic 'translations' in 1762–3

109 The Chief Druid from Henry Rowlands, *Mona Antiqua Restaurata*, 1723, derived from a drawing by Aylett Sammes made from a verbal description of statues believed to be of Druids found in Germany.

seems to have prompted Thomas Percy, later Bishop of Dromore, to publish the contents of a seventeenth-century manuscript of English ballads he had acquired, together with similar poems, as the well-known *Reliques of Ancient English Poetry* in 1765. He had been in correspondence with the Reverend Evan Evans, who as early as 1758 had been collecting Welsh poetry, urging him to produce 'an elegant translation of some curious pieces of ancient British Poetry', which appeared as *Specimens of the Poetry of the Ancient Welsh Bards* the year before Percy's own *Reliques*. Other Welshmen were soon to collect and publish traditional music, notably Edward Jones, whose *Musical and Poetical Relics of the Welsh Bards* came out in 1784, and its second part, *The Bardic Museum of Primitive British Literature*, in 1802. Jones was himself a harper and his collection forms a valuable record of some of the earliest traditional

110 Welsh airs we know: it includes 'A Druidical Song' and closes with a sprightly tune 'Y Derwydd – The Druid'. In Ireland, Charlotte Brooke's *Reliques of Irish Poetry* (1789) acknowledges its debt to Percy in its title.

Evans honestly and sensibly admitted the extreme difficulty he found in translating many of the early poems, but, baffled by the obscurity of some attributed to the sixth-century poet Taliesin, he incautiously claimed that they represented the 'Druid's Caballa'. Iolo went much further, with the advantage that he had no compunction in inventing sources where none existed, and in his *Poems, Lyric and Pastoral* (1794) announced that the poems of Taliesin 'exhibit a complete system of DRUIDISM', and that 'by these (undoubtedly authentic) writings it will appear that the *Ancient British* CHRISTIANITY was strongly tinctured with DRUIDISM'. There is indeed a group of very obscure poems, attributed to Taliesin but more probably of later date, and free 'translations' of these could yield, to Iolo and many others, an unlimited degree of mystic nonsense, but he set the matter on a firm basis of forgery with his thirty 'aphorisms' defining the mysterious doctrines and philosophy of the Druids, allegedly set out in a sixteenth-century manuscript and as unconvincing as the twenty Druid Ordonnances of Noel Taillepied. 'Dedication, learning, self-delusion, mischief and error characterize this phase of Welsh studies,' Dr Owen has sadly written.

Rowland Jones found the Caballistic teaching of the Druids in words and even syllables, and evolved a cosy world of lunatic linguistics in books such as *The Origin of Language and Nations* (1764), *Hieroglyfic* (1768), or *The Circles of Gomer* (1771): we are back among the Children of Gomer, and for Jones, Japhet was himself a Druid. It may be thought surprising to find the author of *Fanny Hill* in such company, but John Cleland had a serious if misguided enthusiasm for linguistics and in *The Way to Things by Words* (1766) he presents Celtic as the parent of all European languages, with primeval wisdom preserved and transmitted by the Druids, who so successfully permeated early Christianity with their doctrines that the Mass took its name not from the words *missa est*,

111, 112 but from the Druids' mistletoe. The Druids had now acquired their own literature, concealed and obscure, but apparent to the eye of faith and recoverable by sympathetic translation, in early Welsh literature; their Patriarchal Religion was reaffirmed in a series of books from William Cooke's *An Enquiry into the Druidical and Patriarchal Religion* (1754) to D. James' *Patriarchal Religion of Britain* (1836), while Edward Davies provided more evidence of deep Druidic lore in his *Celtic Researches* (1804) and *The Mythology and Rites of the British Druids* (1809), which exercised

116, 121 a baleful influence on Meyrick and Smith in their costume book of 1815, and on many others.

Of Rowland Jones it has been written: 'through his influence on the lexicographer William Owen Pughe he helped to pollute the stream of Welsh scholarship throughout the nineteenth century.' With Pughe we enter a very curious world, and one in which the Druids entered the

110 'Y Derwydd – The Druid'. Air for the harp (a jig) from *The Bardic Museum* published by Edward Jones in 1802.

mind of William Blake. The Druids in their latter days begin to move away from scholarship, however eccentric, and offer themselves as symbols within a non-rational universe in which every form of belief and unreason may meet. Pughe was one of the Twenty-four Elders appointed by Joanna Southcott, the religious maniac, together with the engraver William Sharp, who had previously been a follower of Richard Brothers, that engaging character who had announced himself as the 'nephew of the Almighty', descendant of David and ruler of the world: he demanded the surrender of the Crown by George III, and had once met the Devil strolling down Tottenham Court Road. Both Sharp and Pughe were friends of William Blake, and Robert Southey wrote of Pughe, 'Poor Owen found everything he wished to find in the Bardic system, and there he found Blake's notions, and thus Blake and his wife were persuaded that his dreams were old patriarchal truths, long forgotten and now revealed.'

The significance of the appearance of Druids in the text of Blake's *Prophetic Books*, and of versions of Stonehenge and Avebury in the engravings, has been discussed in detail by many writers. Blake had been strongly influenced by the speculative mythologists, especially Bryant in his *New System: or An Analysis of Ancient Mythology* (1774–6): 'the antiquities of every Nation under Heaven', Blake was to write, 'is no less sacred than that of the Jews. They are the same thing, as Jacob Bryant and all antiquaries have proved.' Though the Druids change their character as Blake's own vision changed during the writing of the *Prophetic Books* between 1797 and 1804, they have their apotheosis in the context of his revolutionary discovery that Britain was the original Holy Land, and Jerusalem not so far from Primrose Hill where Iolo had initiated his first Gorsedd. At first Druids are the priests, law-givers, philosophers and mathematicians of Urizen, but by *Jerusalem*, 'All things Begin & End in Albion's Ancient Druid Rocky Shore.' A great Stonehenge trilithon straddles the landscape on one engraved page; on another *114, 115* appears one of 'The Serpent Temples thro' the Earth, from the wide Plain of Salisbury', combining the lintelled peristyle of Stonehenge with

The Celtic Druids.

BY

Godfrey Higgins Esqʳ F.S.A

of Skellow Grange near

Doncaster Yorkshire.

FABRIC OF A VISION

AND LIKE

LEAVE NOT A RACK BEHIND

LONDON.

R. Hunter 72 Sᵗ Pauls Church Yard 1827

111 A romantic title-page, *The Celtic Druids* by Godfrey Higgins, 1827, with Stonehenge in the background.

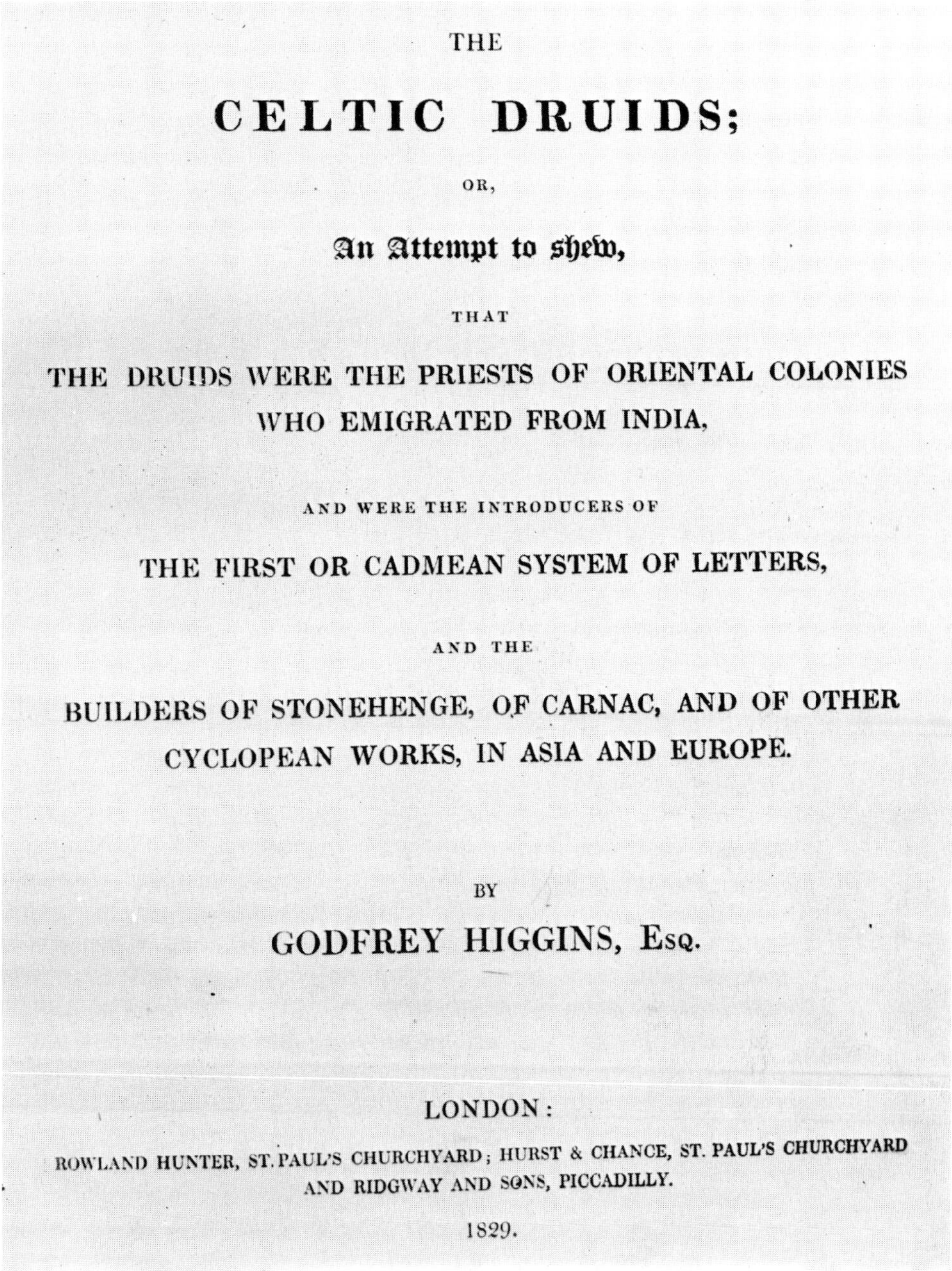

THE

CELTIC DRUIDS;

OR,

An Attempt to shew,

THAT

THE DRUIDS WERE THE PRIESTS OF ORIENTAL COLONIES
WHO EMIGRATED FROM INDIA,

AND WERE THE INTRODUCERS OF

THE FIRST OR CADMEAN SYSTEM OF LETTERS,

AND THE

BUILDERS OF STONEHENGE, OF CARNAC, AND OF OTHER
CYCLOPEAN WORKS, IN ASIA AND EUROPE.

BY

GODFREY HIGGINS, Esq.

LONDON:

ROWLAND HUNTER, ST. PAUL'S CHURCHYARD; HURST & CHANCE, ST. PAUL'S CHURCHYARD
AND RIDGWAY AND SONS, PICCADILLY.

1829.

112 In *The Celtic Druids* Godfrey Higgins linked the Druids to India on
the one hand and to megalithic monuments on the other.

113 The Serpent Temple: engraving forming the final page of William Blake's *Jerusalem* (1804–20) and inspired by Stukeley's imaginative reconstruction of the Avebury circle and avenues, improved by Blake by introducing Stonehenge trilithons. The allegorical figures are Los with hammer and tongs, Vala with a distaff, and probably Luvah.

Stukeley's serpentine version of the Avebury plan. 'The Wicker Man of Scandinavia' is hardly more out of place than Edward Gibbon's belief that the *Edda* was the sacred book of the Celts: many were confusing and conflating the pagan priesthoods of northern Europe. 'Was Britain the Primitive Seat of the Patriarchal Religion?' Blake asked, and straightway gave his answer: Patriarchal Druids originated in Britain and spread their doctrine far and wide, even to the oak-groves on the Plain of Mamre. 'Your Ancestors,' he told his readers, 'derived their origin from Abraham, Heber, Shem and Noah, who were Druids, as the Druid Temples (which are Patriarchal Pillars and Oak Groves) over the whole Earth witness to this day.' And in a single phrase Blake takes us, and the Druids, back to a familiar landscape. 'The Nature of my Work,' he wrote, 'is Visionary or Imaginative; it is an endeavour to Restore what the Ancients call'd the Golden Age.'

DRUIDS IN DECLINE

The nineteenth century shows us two main strands in the decadence of Druid folk-lore. On the one hand, the venerable priests remained as innocuous or even half-frivolous figures of romantic antiquity who could act as stock characters in landscape or literature. Already in the eighteenth century natural features such as 'rocking stones' or eccentric-

114 A Mythological Trilithon, from William Blake's *Jerusalem*, Chap. 3, 70. There are many references to Druids and Stonehenge, and here a vast trilithon, based on those of Stonehenge, dominates a landscape and 'the Oak Groves of Albion'. The three figures seem to be Bacon, Newton and Locke.

ally weathered outcrops were being claimed as objects of Druidic veneration; the Cheesewring (or Wringcheese) in Cornwall for instance, claimed for the Druids by William Borlase in his *Antiquities of Cornwall* (1754) together with most of the visible pre-Christian monuments of the Duchy. A similar weathered block, the Agglestone in the Isle of Purbeck, was also being regarded as 'originally a heathen Altar, made use of by the Druids for sacrificial purposes' by an antiquary writing as late as 1856. In 1773, Druids and mistletoe appear with a natural rock
117 stack at Rishworth in the West Riding of Yorkshire; here too the Idol Rock at Brimham near Harrogate was to be acclaimed a Druid sanctuary,
118 while not far away, at Ilton near Masham, William Danby of Swinton Hall built, in the 1820's, not only an artificial Cheesewring, but an eccentric and magnificent Druid Temple, complete with trilithons: this striking folly is 'rediscovered' from time to time (up to 1951 at least) as
115 an unrecorded prehistoric megalithic monument. At Park Place, near Henley-on-Thames, General Conway in 1788 re-erected a megalithic monument which had stood at St Helier until the grateful inhabitants of Jersey presented it to him on his retiring from the Governorship of the island: it is adorned with a French inscription describing it as an 'ancien Temple des Druides'.

Actual dressed-up Druids could appear, too, in the more ambitious schemes of landscape gardening, in rivalry with what Edith Sitwell called Ancient and Ornamental Hermits. Sir Rowland Hill, inventor of the Penny Post, had one installed at Hawkstone in Shropshire, who

115 Megalithic monument transported from Jersey in 1788 and re-erected at Park Place, Henley-on-Thames, from Britton and Brayley, *Beauties of England and Wales*, 1802.

116 An Archdruid in his Judicial Habit, coloured acquatint from Meyrick and Smith, *The Costume of the Original Inhabitants of the British Isles*, 1815, with Irish Bronze Age antiquities and a mystical snake (from Taliesin).

117 Druid, Rocking Stone and Mistletoe at Rishworth,
West Riding, Yorkshire, 1773.

startled visitors by appearing 'with a hoary and laurelled head made to
look yet more awesome by the light thrown on his face from a pale
green glass', and the elaborate garden lay-out also included an 'Otaheitan
Cottage, fitted up in a very appropriate stile', as an appreciative visitor
recorded in 1802: Druids and the South Seas nicely met again. With a
fine confusion of folk-lore, the folly known as Robin Hood's Temple at
Halsewell in Somerset was described at much the same time as 'a Druid's
Temple in a just style of Bark, etc., the view quite gloomy and confined'.
Early in the nineteenth century, too, George Henry Law, Bishop of
Bath and Wells, constructed a notable folly-garden at Banwell in the
Mendips, in which was a Bone Cave entered by Gothic arches and
containing the inscription:

> Here where once druids trod in times of yore
> And stain'd their altars with a victim's gore,
> Here now the Christian ransomed from above
> Adores a God of mercy and of love.

As romantic adornments, Druids were now hackneyed figures in minor
verse and prose. Sir Richard Colt Hoare of Stourhead was one of the first

118 Drawing by Barbara Jones of the Megalithic Folly at Ilton,
West Riding, Yorkshire.

great field archaeologists of his time, and the epigraph to his *Ancient
Wiltshire* (1812) is WE SPEAK FROM FACTS, NOT THEORY, but
he could not resist printing a poem by his friend the Reverend William
Lisle Bowles, occasioned by a thunderstorm while digging a barrow,
which inevitably included 'The white-hair'd Druid bard sublime'.
English romanticism was soon taking a hold on the imagination in more
than one European country, and on Boxing Day 1831 Bellini's opera
Norma was produced at La Scala: the main characters are Druidic, and

119 Cover illustration on sheet music of a quadrille arranged by Charles d'Albert, showing Norma and her father the Archdruid, with Stonehenge in the background.

120 Scene from a modern production of Bellini's *Norma* (at La Scala, Milan, 1964–5) with a 'megalithic' stage set by Salvatore Fiume.

121 Druids as illustrated by S. R. Meyrick and C. H. Smith in 1815, based on an eighteenth-century engraving by Montfaucon of a Gallo-Roman relief (not of Druids) from Autun.

the scene is set in Gaul. Ten years later Angelo Catelani, a pupil of Donizetti, produced in Modena his opera *Carattaco* on an Ancient British theme which must have included Druids. The first performance of *Norma* took place in front of a conventional classical trompe-l'oeil backcloth, as Sanquirico's contemporary drawing shows, but in England by the early 1840's, when the title role was sung by Adelaide Kemble, daughter of Charles Kemble the actor and sister of J. M. Kemble the Anglo-Saxon scholar, Stonehenge appeared, and it is shown again on the contemporary music-sheets of the opera.

119, 120

Side-by-side with this decorative Druidry, in which prehistory was light-heartedly plundered as an alternative to Gothick or Chinoiserie, there ran a strain of more erratic and odd Druidism developing from the mystical nonsense extracted from misinterpreted Welsh texts. Such books as that by Edward Davies already mentioned not only influenced a romantic and credulous public, but were thought worthy of attention or refutation by apparently reputable academics such as the Reverend Algernon Herbert, Dean of Merton College Oxford, who in his

122 Portrait of Dr William Price of Llantrisant, wearing a 'suit of scarlet merino wool with green silk lettering', forming the frontispiece to his *Gwylellis yn Nayd* (The Will of My Father), 1871.

123 Cremation of Dr William Price at East Caerlan, Llantrisant, 1893.

Neodruidic Heresy in Britannia (1838) scented out, as his title implies, heretical Druids in the early Christian Church. In spite of a few pieces of astringent criticism, such as that provided by D. W. Nash in his *Taliesin* of 1858, what strikes one in almost all the contemporary writing on the subject is the reckless disregard for anything approaching a critical handling of the source material. On Celtic philology an almost unrelieved lunatic darkness had fallen for the century and a half between Edward Lhwyd and the *Grammatica Celtica* of the German scholar Zeuss, which appeared in 1853.

The speculative mythologists held their own in some quarters, and particularly in Wales, where Pontypridd in Glamorgan seems to have had a peculiarly rich Druidic nineteenth century, appropriate to a town in Iolo's own county, and one in which he was said to have performed his ritual at, inevitably, a Rocking Stone. The appearance there of Dr William Price of Llantrisant as a Druid was bound to raise things to a high pitch of eccentricity. Price, born in 1800, lived to be 93, and is best *122* remembered for his trial at Cardiff Assizes for cremating his son, whom he had named Iesu Grist, on his death aged five months in 1884; he was acquitted and was himself cremated in 1893. His Druidic costume owed *123* nothing to tradition: in white tunic, scarlet waistcoat and green trousers, *124* and with a fox's skin on his head and shoulders, he must have been a colourful figure as he chanted 'a song of the primitive Bard to the Moon'

124 Dr William Price [of Llantrisant] in another costume, wearing his fox-skin cap and carrying a torch and a moon symbol.

at the Rocking Stone. This natural feature was 'improved', probably about 1860 by the local bard Myfyr Morganwg, by the addition of stones in a serpentine setting, and so made more authentically Druidic. Another local bard, Owen Morgan or Morien, carried on the tradition of nonsense at Pontypridd until his death in 1921: he managed to reconcile his pious Welsh Calvinistic Methodism with Druidism even though it meant equating Taliesin with Jesus Christ, and he published curious, locally printed, undated, books towards the end of the nineteenth century which might have been written a hundred years or more earlier. Each has several alternative titles, such as *Kimmerian Revelations or the Royal Winged Son of Stonehenge and Avebury*, or *The Light of Britannia*, with five subtitles ranging from Phallic Worship to the Holy Greal, by way of Druidic Mysteries. And in keeping with its ripe history of Druidic eccentricity, it was fittingly at the Pontypridd Eisteddfod of

125 Modern Druids celebrating the Summer Solstice at Stonehenge, June 1968. The ritual properties in the foreground include a rose, and a copper globe in which a flame is ignited.

126 The induction of Mr Winston Churchill into the Albion Lodge of the Ancient Order of Druids at Blenheim, 15 August 1908. The false beards suggest that the occasion was perhaps not wholly serious.

1878 that the Archdruid, in addition to the normal Gorsedd ceremony, should have offered prayers to that sinister Hindu deity, Kali.

The Welsh Druids, corporate in the Eisteddfod or crazily individual, were however not alone. Already in 1781 a 'secret' society, the Ancient Order of Druids, had been set up in London by Henry Hurle, a carpenter and builder in business on Garlick Hill in the City, on lines doubtless inspired by Freemasonry. It was not primarily a Benefit Society, though help to impoverished members was implicit in its constitution, but in 1833 the Order split on this question, and a majority seceded to form a straightforward charitable institution under the title of The United Ancient Order of Druids. This, with a widespread international series of daughter Orders, flourishes as a Friendly Society today, but the rump of the 1833 split also continued on its original mystical lines. Represented by the Albion Lodge of the Ancient Order of Druids of Oxford, it
126   accepted as an initiate the young Winston Churchill at a ceremony in Blenheim Park in August 1908. In considering this Order, and the other

bodies of self-styled Druids which today represent the fag-end of the myth, we enter a world at once misleading and rather pathetic. We may begin our sad pilgrimage through error once again at Stonehenge.

The monument before 1900 was in private hands and stood unfenced on lonely downland. Druid bodies of some sort were certainly holding ceremonies there by the end of the last century, but the nature of these organizations, then and today, impermanent and liable to the constant secession and fission incident to small sects, and without critical standards as applied to their own history, makes investigation virtually impossible. The fall of one of the Stonehenge uprights in 1900 caused the owner, Sir Edward Antrobus, to fence the monument and to charge entry, and a contretemps then ensued at the next Solstice ceremony, when the chief Druid was ejected by the police, and publicly and ritually cursed Sir Edward. In 1915 Stonehenge was sold (for £6,600) to Mr (later Sir Cecil) Chubb, who presented it to the nation with a Government ceremony at

127 Stonehenge Forsaken: the Order of Bards, Ovates and Druids have left Stonehenge in favour of other sites believed to be of mystic importance, including Tower Hill in London, where this procession took place in March 1964.

which Druids also assisted. One group called the Druid Hermetists had performed there before the First World War, and since 1919, when Stonehenge became a national monument under the Ancient Monuments Acts, at least five different bodies of Druids have been in correspondence with the Ancient Monuments Inspectorate. It is said that at the beginning of the century a dissident sect, led by Lady Poore, celebrated rites at a Bronze Age disc-barrow on her land south of Stonehenge, in pique at her not having been elected Chief of the original body. By 1949 the Stonehenge celebrants were reduced by two groups, holding their assemblies on different days around the Summer Solstice, and from 1955 only one has appeared. Of these, that which has now withdrawn seems to have represented the minority group of Henry Hurle's original Order; the survivor, The British Circle of the Universal Bond, has again suffered secession with the formation of The Order of Bards, Ovates and Druids in 1963, who have forsaken Stonehenge in favour of ceremonies on Tower Hill in London and at the Early Iron Age hill-fort of Hunsbury near Northampton.

127

It is a strange little story of decline and fall. The Universal Bond, without being able to produce documentation, claimed direct descent from a mythical meeting of British Druids organized in 1717 by (of all people) John Toland at (of all places) Primrose Hill, and to have continued under the successive chieftainship of such as William Stukeley, Lord Winchilsea and William Blake, up to the present. In recent times it certainly attracted colourful characters, the most notable being the Chief Druid from 1909 to 1946, George Watson MacGregor Reid, friend of Bernard Shaw and one of the few people to have stood, unsuccessfully, for both the United States Senate and the House of Commons, and who was the reputed original of Dr Nikola in Guy Boothby's still-remembered thrillers of the early years of this century.

125

The Stonehenge sunrise ceremonies of recent years attracted irresponsible crowds of sightseers and were the occasion of deplorable acts of hooliganism, and since 1964 the public have been excluded from the Druids' dawn performances. The ritual of both groups is vaguely mystical, couched in terms so colourless as to offend no religious susceptibilities of any kind; the Ancient Order sang etiolated versions of Hymns Ancient and Modern to a harmonium accompaniment, giving a faint flavour of Nonconformist pietism, and the ceremonies of both bodies inspire a mood of gentle ridicule rather than awed respect. As we watch them we have come a very long way from the Druids of Posidonius or Lucan, and almost as far, by way of Primrose Hill and Garlick Hill, from the ideas of Aubrey and Stukeley in which the present ceremonies at Stonehenge had their origin.

Chapter Five
EPILOGUE

DRUIDS AS FACT AND AS SYMBOL

Our main task of investigation is now over. In three chapters we have considered, first, the nature of the early Celtic society in which the existence of Druids is recorded from the beginning of the second century BC; second, the literary evidence in the relevant classical and vernacular sources on which our knowledge of Druids is based; and finally the creation, from the Renaissance to the present day, of Druid myth and folk-lore. It will have become clear to the reader that we have had to deal with two kinds of Druids, the products of either objective or of subjective thinking: Druids-as-known and Druids-as-wished-for, Druids as fact and Druids as symbol. In this final short chapter, by way of an Epilogue, we may conveniently bring together some of the strands of fact and inference, and consider them in their appropriate contexts. We may first look at Druids as Fact: the priesthood of that name of which we have cognisance in antiquity. These were the real Druids, and as such demand a rather more detailed discussion of their position in ancient European religion than we have so far attempted.

It must be remembered that this is a book about the Druids, and not a study of the pagan Celtic religion of which, in their factual aspect, they were among the priests. With very few exceptions, all treatments of the religion of the Celts have suffered from the ignorance of their authors of European prehistory, and of the archaeological evidence on which this is in large part based. In earlier studies, this was excusable, since the structure of European prehistory had not then been worked out, and the techniques of the recovery and interpretation of archaeological evidence had not been refined, but today this excuse can no longer be offered. Celtic religion, and with it, the Druids, have been treated *in vacuo* without any attempt to set the religious practices and beliefs of Early Iron Age Gaul and Britain within the framework of the cultures of which they are an expression. Religion is a social artifact, just as are language and literature, houses and pots, domesticated animals or the working of metals. It is brought into being within a society to fulfil certain psychological needs, and is intimately bound up with custom and law, the hierarchies of social structure and the proper functioning of the institutions which define and hold in coherence the society itself. The nature of the early Celtic world is documented by archaeology and by texts; furthermore it came into being after a long antecedent prehistory, the main structure of which can be reasonably inferred from the evidence of material culture. It is to be hoped that an historian of religion will before long take up the problem in realistic terms, and examine the Celtic situation in the light of all available source-material. In the meantime, a very sketchy outline of some possibilities which should be borne in mind is given here as a framework within which to set the factual Druids of antiquity, Druids Discovered by modern scholarship. It should be repeated, however, that we are making more assumptions than inferences.

Direct equations between material culture, which is the subject-matter of archaeology and consequently the foundation of prehistory, and forms of religion, which can only be known from texts, is impossible if the latter do not exist. We looked at some of the problems presented in chapter I, when we saw, however, that some part of inferences may in some circumstances be made, and as assumptions perhaps rather more often, provided we always remember that in so doing we are, to quote Atkinson's words again, 'indulging in speculation upon subjects about which there is no possibility of greater certainty'. In these guarded terms some speculations are offered here as possible indications of lines of further investigation, in the hope that it may stimulate those more qualified.

DRUIDS DISCOVERED

The position of the Druids in European prehistory renders it improbable that their religion, like their material culture and by inference other aspects of their social and linguistic situation, did not draw on a long past of varied cultural traditions, not all necessarily Celtic nor even Indo-European. What we can perceive of early Celtic religion through text-aided archaeology will then be something already embodying an ancient tradition, and we must be on the look-out for possible signs of syncretism. There is a long prehistory behind the Druids: *vixere fortes ante Diviciacum.*

The basic European cultures from the Late Glacial period up to about the sixth millennium BC were based on the subsistence-economics of hunting, fishing and food-collecting which collectively comprehend the Advanced Palaeolithic and Mesolithic cultures. In some areas of northern Eurasia such cultural traditions had a long persistence side-by-side with those of intrusive agriculturists, probably up to the end of the third millennium BC. In their essentials, such cultures lie behind those of the original inhabitants of the New World, who had crossed the Bering Straits from Asia from around 10,000 BC.

More than one historian of religion has suggested that equations might be made between such cultures and that type of archaic ecstatic religion which has survived until recent times in the Old and New World under the name of shamanism. The form in which extreme advocacy of this view has been made does not in all cases inspire confidence in the writers' handling of archaeological evidence, but as a general thesis cautiously advanced by such as Mircea Eliade it seems worth serious consideration. It would among other things explain the recent distribution of shamanism, particularly in Siberia and America – among Tungus, Buriats, Altaians and Lapps, and from Eskimos through Chuckchees and Crees to Tierra del Fuego. It need not have been the whole content of Palaeolithic and Mesolithic religion but it could have been an important component, and one that could form a substrate in the ancient European tradition.

From the seventh or sixth millennium B C a decisive cultural change in eastern Europe was precipitated by the introduction of economies based on domesticated animals and cereal crops, with their general origin in the Near East. The mechanics of transmission are still obscure but need not concern us here; whether by immigration or acculturation or both, a complex of ideas including the practice of mixed farming, village communities of one-roomed houses with mud or timber walls, set in a loose open plan, and a series of new skills including at an early stage the making of pottery, was implanted in Europe. Its origins lay in the same peasant communities as were, in Western Asia, to develop into precocious literate civilizations by the end of the fourth millennium B C, but unlike the oriental cultures, which early developed the monumental temple as a focus of the settlement, nothing which could be interpreted in such terms has been detected in those of the first stone-using agriculturists in East and Central Europe. In their essentials the Neolithic villages of continental Europe, and the economy they represent, lie behind all subsequent prehistory, modified only by the successive technological increments of working copper, bronze, and finally iron. In a restricted area of East Europe the occurrence of female figurines in the settlement debris has led to unverifiable assumptions about the cult of a Mother Goddess; in Western Europe an alien and unknown set of beliefs must have been involved in the building of megalithic or rock-cut collective tombs, some adorned with stylized female representations. We are in fact ignorant of what may well have been many varieties of religious experience among the European Neolithic communities from the sixth to the late third millennium B C, and their potential contribution to later Celtic religion is a wholly unknown factor.

The end of the third millennium B C was a period of change and readjustment in Europe. We see the end of the archaic phase of stone-using agricultural communities not only in the technological shift from stone to copper and bronze for edge-tools and weapons, but in changes which may imply social re-alignments: the long houses which had characterized the Central European tradition from the fifth millennium B C, which could plausibly be explained in terms of 'extended' or 'undivided' family units, now give way to buildings appropriate to the 'nuclear' family of the early Celtic world and of modern Western Europe. Although the nature of the movements involved are still a matter of lively discussion, there is certainly evidence of some sort of contacts extending from the region of the South Russian steppe and the Caucasus, north-westwards into Central and Northern Europe before 2000 BC, including, it now seems likely, the first knowledge of wheeled transport with paired draught animals, and the rite of burying a vehicle with the dead.

These movements and changes have been associated with the dispersal of Indo-European languages, and while as in all correlations between language and material culture in non-literate contexts this is an assumption, it would be consistent with the picture later presented when linguistic distributions can be defined. So far as the area later to become Celtic Europe is concerned, we can do no more than suggest that by the opening of the second millennium BC there could have been speakers of Indo-European languages already establishing themselves, and that Celtic in some form could have been one of these. If we make another assumption, we could go on to add Indo-European social, institutional and religious patterns, if such can indeed be thought to have existed as a distinctively common feature before the diaspora. Whatever may be felt about this early dating, we have in the archaeological evidence good reason to infer no marked cultural change before the period when Celtic is first recorded at least as far back as the eighth, and probably to the thirteenth century BC, so that the linguistic situation may be supposed to be similarly unbroken, and even to be of greater antiquity.

By the time of the historically documented Druids the background of possible religious tradition would then be roughly as follows. Taking as a starting-point the forms of Celtic religion as inferred from archaeology, epigraphy and the classical and vernacular texts, there are three main antecedent phases. The first would be the traditions, predominantly Indo-European, going back to the second millennium BC and perhaps to its beginnings. Behind this again would be the wholly obscure religions of the Neolithic agriculturists with, in Gaul and especially Britain, eastern and western components mixed from the end of the fourth millennium BC. And finally, underlying all, there would be the beliefs and rites of the hunting peoples of pre-agricultural Europe which might well have contained elements surviving in shamanism. It is a pedigree which could be a good 20,000 years in length.

Druidism, when we first encounter it, is an integral part of the social structure of Celtic Gaul; it is an Indo-European institution with, whatever criticisms may be levelled against the over-elaborate schemes of Dumézil and his school, analogues in the Brahmin class of Sanskrit India or the archaic priesthoods of early Rome. But there are distinctive elements which may owe their existence to those earlier sources of European religious tradition we have just sketched out. We can reasonably read the archaeological evidence to imply the existence of a social order of the 'heroic' type well back into the second millennium BC, with rites such as the vehicle-burial later current, in certainly Celtic contexts, in the wagon-graves of Hallstatt and the chariot-graves of La Tène. In such a social situation a priestly class equivalent to Druids, no less than bards and vaticinators, would have an appropriate place. The ritual shafts of

128

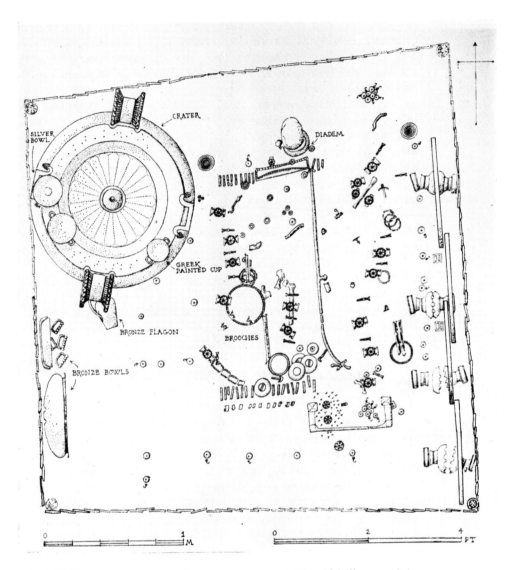

128 A Hallstatt wagon-grave of a young woman at Vix, Châtillon-sur-Seine, France, with imported Greek bronze vessels, sixth century BC.

the Celtic world have, as we saw, antecedents in middle second-millennium Britain, where too the tradition of the circular shrine or delimited *temenos* area goes back ever farther. The elongated Celtic sanctuary-enclosure of Libenice has its best parallel in France early in the first millennium BC, and the square shrine has similar antecedents in the Low Countries.

The possible contributions from the earliest agricultural traditions in the Celtic areas, which can by no means be allied to Indo-European ideas, are virtually impossible to analyse. Inferences as to social organization before the beginning of the second millennium in Gaul or Britain can only be so hazardous as to be nugatory. We can only draw attention to a distinct Gaulish 'interest' in megalithic tombs, with inserted burials and what looks like more than picnic debris deposited in them; and in Britain, to the possible antecedents of circular, square and elongated ceremonial enclosures in those of the henge and cursus type going back well into the third millennium B C.

'We do not believe it possible to find in shamanism the dominant in the magico-religious life of the Indo-Europeans,' Eliade has written, even if, as he points out, some speakers of Indo-European languages such as the Thracians, and above all the Scyths, incorporated many shamanistic practices into their religion. It is difficult to accept Anne Ross's view that the Druids were 'priests who do not seem to have differed so very basically from the shamans of the Finno-Ugric peoples', though she quotes from a vernacular Irish text, the *Siege of Drom Damhghaire*, a significant episode. Here the great Munster Druid, Mogh Ruith, is depicted as a wizard and magician who calls for his 'dark grey hornless bull-hide' and his 'white-speckled bird headpiece with its fluttering wings' in which he makes a very shamanistic flight into the air. Here, and in the other ritual and ecstatic contexts of the use of bull-hides, we may indeed have a fragment from a very archaic substrate of belief. Here too we might place such evidence as the sacrificial deposits of horse-hides or ox-hides, represented by the surviving skulls and leg-bones, recently identified in the votive find at La Tène itself: this 'heads-and-hoofs' practice, known from the late third millennium B C onwards in South Russia, was a feature of recent shamanism in the Altai and elsewhere. If any weight is given to the apparent common usage between the Celts and the Turkic peoples of a proverbial saying about earth and heaven opening, which we noted in chapter III, a curious link with the Central Asia would be implicit.

The factual Druids were, then, the members of an Indo-European social order, practising a religion which may have contained many elements already ancient in their day. We know of them because other people, of alien cultural traditions, wrote about them: they are Druids Observed. And in the process of observation, symbolic Druids, Druids-as-wished-for, first make their appearance.

DRUIDS OBSERVED

The knowledge of Druids acquired by the classical world moved over the years from reality to unreality, as encounter was diluted into report, and report faded into rumour. Druids were directly encountered, probably by Posidonius and certainly by Caesar; Cicero, somehow surmounting the language barrier, talked philosophy with Diviciacus; Suetonius Paulinus and his army were publicly cursed by Druids on the shores of the Menai Straits. Straightforward copying of standard sources brought the Druids by report into the writings of those who had not travelled in Celtic lands, and in the final phases, the Druids, by now rumour only, were picked up with other miscellaneous ethnographical and philosophical oddments by the Alexandrian scholars and the early Church fathers.

Even from the first the Druids were inevitably the victims of the interests and ideologies of those who observed them. Posidonius was looking hopefully for confirmation of his ideas of an age of innocence and virtuous law-giving philosophers in a landscape gilded with reflections from a Golden Age; Caesar was also looking hopefully, but over his shoulder to his political prestige in Rome. But on the whole the writings of the Posidonian group give us a remarkably objective picture of the Druids, and of the Celtic culture of which they were an expression. The authenticity of the picture they present is vouched for by its close coincidence with those obtained from the vernacular sources, and from archaeological evidence. By the time we come to Druids as rumour, they were sufficiently remote from real knowledge to be shaped into whatever form was needed, and what was needed was intuitive philosophers, unspoiled children of nature who could walk close to the gods and even instruct Pythagoras in esoteric wisdom.

Light-heartedly, C. S. Calverley opened his *Ode to Beer* with the words:

> In those old days which poets say were golden
> Perhaps they laid the gilding on themselves;
> And, if they did, I'm all the more beholden
> To those brown dwellers on my dusty shelves . . .

But in thus linking the imagined Golden Age of classical antiquity with the tooled leather of book-bindings on the library shelf the lines take us appropriately enough, in our pursuit of Druids, from the ancient world to the calf-bound folios of Sammes or Stukeley, and the acrid dust collecting on Rowland Jones or Edward Davies. We move from Druids Observed to Druids Imagined.

DRUIDS IMAGINED

The soft radiance of the Golden Age has shone as a constant comfort and an equally constant delusion to many men from Homer to today: it has burnt clear for a millennium longer than the lamp in Tullia's tomb, 'untouch'd for fifteen hundred year'. Seneca tells us how Posidonius looked for the Golden Age; Arthur Barlowe found it among the American Indians that many of his time compared with the Ancient Britons; William Blake placed it firmly on Albion's Ancient Druid Rocky Shore. From the Renaissance onwards, successive generations, rediscovered the Golden Age whenever need for it arose: golden ages too can be socially desirable artifacts. Druids sometimes walked in the enchanted landscape; grave philosophers among Noble Savages; stern champions of Liberty; the sages of Natural Religion or Patriarchs attentive to God's own Word. In another mood Druids could figure as characters of terror, performing, against a backcloth by Salvator Rosa, gory and obscene

129 Painting by Holman Hunt (1827–1910), *A Christian Missionary Sheltering from the Druids*. The missionary is being tended in a very pre-Raphaelite setting, while Druids perform their rites at a stone circle or chase another missionary across the corn-plot.

sacrifices; Druids as 'really horrid' as Catherine Morland or any other reader of Gothick novels could wish. Like the American Indians or the Polynesians with whom they were from time to time compared, the Ancient Britons and their Druid priests could be viewed in terms of either hard or soft primitivism. Again, for those who wished to move with excited incomprehension in a dark world of mysteries revealed in mistranslated Welsh, Druids sired by Iolo out of Taliesin were there to offer delusive assistance. And in the ceremonies of the Gorsedd and at the Stonehenge Summer Solstice, corporate Druidry could be a rallying: point for nationalistic fervour or for shared vagaries of minority beliefs, and an opportunity, in a world starved of ceremonial, for dressing-up and putting on an act.

129, 130

The public appeal of the Druids, especially as an Ancient People connected with Stonehenge and other monuments, is not difficult to understand. In the later nineteenth century antiquaries were becoming archaeologists, and in the lecture room or at county archaeological societies' excursions, they were exorcising the Druids from their new model of the past, the Ages of Stone, Bronze and Iron. With increasing knowledge of prehistory has come the need for other models of greater complexity, but no escape from the essential anonymity of the non-literate past. The ordinary man, finding himself in an arid, unreal world of cultures, periods and typologies, turns with relief to people with a name, and instinctively prefers simplistic explanations of complex problems. The Druids make comfortably comprehensible, historical people like The Roundheads, The Crusaders or The Romans, and to attribute Stonehenge to them makes a sort of sense, as a welcome cliché grasped because it avoids the necessity of thought.

The Druids have brought us once again to Stonehenge. 'Every age,' Jacquetta Hawkes has recently written, 'has the Stonehenge it deserves – or desires.' It was a romantic eighteenth century that desired Druids at Stonehenge, and so they began their long connection with the monument, taking over from Geoffrey of Monmouth's Merlin, Inigo Jones's Romans, and Dr Charleton's Danes. But as she pointed out in her brilliant review of a current controversy, today's Stonehenge-as-wished-for is, in accordance with changing fashions in man's hierarchies and scales of value, a scientific instrument. Can we dare hope that the Druids will once more come into their own, backed by a fine confusion of Hyperborean myth and the lasting bronze of the Coligny Calendar, and that our own age too may have the Druids it desires, who, white robes exchanged for white laboratory coats will be astronomers writing computer programmes in Gallo-Brittonic?

130 Druids in the Vineyard: the wines of Bergerac in the Dordogne include one bottled at the Château du Chayne, and with chayne = chêne = oak, it is labelled as the 'Vin des Druides', with an appropriate design.

NOTES ON THE TEXT

CHAPTER I

Certain basic works have been used throughout this book; of these, Kendrick 1927, though necessarily out-of-date archaeologically, is still the best treatment. The older works of Dottin (1906) and d'Arbois de Joubainville (1906) are still of value for comment on the texts and general good sense. The same cannot be said of some more recent summary statements; le Roux 1961 suffers from ignorance of the relevant prehistory and an uncritical use of late vernacular sources. Chadwick 1966 discusses important material from the classical sources but maintains a position hardly justified by the evidence. For archaeology, Powell 1958; Schwarz 1962; Piggott 1965; de Laet 1966; Ross 1967 all deal directly or indirectly with such problems. The classical texts relating to Celtic religion are printed in the original languages in Zwicker 1934; most of those referring to the Druids (texts and translations), in Kendrick 1927; Tierney 1960; Chadwick 1966. Recent general treatments of Celtic religion from the textual and iconographic sources include Vendryes 1948; Lambrechts 1942; 1954; Duval 1957; de Vries 1963; Ross 1967. The status of the early Irish sources is set out in Jackson 1964, and general consideration of the early antiquarian redis-covery of the Druids in Kendrick 1927; Piggott 1950 and Owen 1962.

The quotations on the nature of archaeological evidence are from Atkinson 1960; Hawkes 1954; Wheeler 1950; Smith 1955; Ucko 1962 and Fox 1959; on the emotive interpretation of iconography from Toynbee 1964; Richmond 1956 and Kendrick 1938; on the British and Gaulish languages from Jackson 1953.

CHAPTER II

Recent treatments of the Celtic world using up-to-date evidence are in Powell 1958; Filip 1962; Hawkes 1963 and Piggott 1965, with biblio-graphies. In the field of technology note now also Driehaus 1965 (iron-working), and Müller-Wille 1965 and Fowler & Evans 1967 (agriculture and field-systems). For the social order, in Gaul cf. Holmes 1911; Hawkes 1957; in early Ireland, Binchy 1943; 1954; 1961; Greene 1954; Tierney 1960; Jackson 1964. Lan-guage and literacy in Jackson 1953; Evans 1967; papyrus, Wild 1966 (but contra, Hodges 1966); Allen 1971.

For shrines and temples in general, for Europe, Schwarz 1962; Piggott 1965; de Laet 1966; for Britain, Lewis 1966; Ross 1967 (all with full references). The quotation is from

Koebner 1941. Shrines at Trier, etc., Steiner 1935. The original Heidenmauer excavations are in Forrer 1899 and new results in Rieth 1958. Rectangular enclosures, Schwarz 1962; Stead 1961; Wallertheim, Behrens 1930; Bokerly Dyke, Pitt-Rivers 1892; Casterley, Cunnington 1914; Jansová 1968; new shrines at South Cadbury, Alcock 1972.

Ritual shafts, Schwarz 1962; Piggott 1963; Ashbee 1963; Long Wittenham, Haverfield 1900; Bosence, Fox 1964; Gundestrup scene, Kimmig 1965; wells and votive deposits, Ross 1967; Jankuhn 1970. Wooden figures, Martin 1965; Vatin 1972; distribution of local cults, Lambrechts 1942; Lingones will, Hatt 1951. For the tripartite nature of function in Indo-European society and religion, Dumézil 1935, and summary of detail set out in many other studies, 1952.

CHAPTER III

The Greek and Latin texts will be found in Zwicker 1934; Kendrick 1927; Tierney 1960 and Chadwick 1966. The main discussion of primitivism and Noble Savages in antiquity is in Lovejoy & Boas 1935; for the Golden Age, Baldry 1952; Griffiths 1956; Guthrie 1957; Phillips 1964. The Hyperboreans are also considered in these works and in Dottin 1906, and the quotation on Aristeas is from Bolton 1962; Dodds 1951 discusses Abaris. The relationships of the Posidonian group of sources are set out in Tierney 1960, and the Alexandrian tradition in Chadwick 1966. The comment on Caesar's literary style is from Grant 1958. For reactions between Romans and the Druids, de Witt 1938.

The most up-to-date statement on the pre-Christian Irish tales is the short study by Jackson (1964), where the status of the Irish Druids is also touched on, as also in Binchy 1954, 1961, and in Greene 1954. The title

of *gutuater* is dealt with by Evans (1967), and for the historical status of the *Scriptores Historiae Augustae*, Momigliano 1966a. Mircea Eliade (1954) has discussed the *omphalos* concept in early religion. A recent study of the *vates* is that of Köves (1955); for Pythagoras and Zalmoxis, Kirk & Raven 1957; Dodds 1951. Szabo (1965) notes the literal aspect of Celtic immortality, and the quotations are from Richmond 1950, who instances the Simpelveld sarcophagus.

For the Coligny Calendar, MacNeill 1928; Powell 1958; among recent studies, Daviet 1963. Ancient calendar-making in Nilsson 1920; Neugebauer 1957, with Tamil astronomy, 1952. The quotation from Jordanes is from the translation in Mierow 1966; on Jordanes and Cassiodorus, Momigliano 1966b. Celtic proverbial sayings, Jackson 1964; Orkhon River inscription, Bowra 1964.

The Roman proscriptions of the Druids have often been discussed; cf. de Witt 1938; Chadwick 1966. For the Irish and the Elizabethans, Quinn 1966. Last's views (1949) are quoted here; on the 'Moral Barrier', Alföldi 1952.

CHAPTER IV

For general treatments of antiquarianism in Britain from the Middle Ages to the eighteenth century, Kendrick 1950; Piggott 1950, 1951, 1956, 1967; for Druids in this context, Kendrick 1927; Owen 1962, and for Annius, with Kendrick 1950. The writers on Druids up to the earlier eighteenth century are listed, excerpted and in part reprinted in Frick 1744.

The impact of the discovery of man in the Americas and Polynesia is discussed by Hodgen (1964) and in the context of Noble Savages by Fairchild (1961). Additional quotations on early and primitive man are in Slotkin 1965; Ireland in Quinn 1966; John

White's and other early drawings of Ancient Britons in Kendrick 1950; Utopianism, Manuel 1965. I have adopted the spelling *Boudica* on Professor Jackson's advice, as in his note in Dudley & Webster 1962; cf. also Evans s.v.

The eighteenth-century admiration of groves is set out in Lovejoy 1948b, c. A bibliography of 947 items relating to Stonehenge to the date of compilation is in Harrison 1901; cf. Atkinson 1960a. For Wood and his buildings in Bath, Summerson 1949; Stukeley, Piggott 1950; Natural Religion and Deism, Willey 1940; Lovejoy 1948a; Noble Savages, Fairchild 1961. Scottish Primitivists and others, Lovejoy 1936; Whitney 1934; Piggott 1955. Druids and megalithic monuments in France, Daniel 1960.

For the Gorsedd and Edward Williams, Peate 1951; Daniel 1961; Matthew Arnold (1867) describes the Llandudno Eisteddfod. There is a large literature on Blake and the Druids, summarized in Owen 1962, to which add Todd 1946. The association of Druids with follies and natural rocks is touched on in Jones 1953; Palmer 1964 and Moir 1964. Mr Michael Ayrton has helped me on *Norma* and *Caratacco*. Pontypridd, Dr Price and Morien, Denning 1963; Daniel 1970. The early circumstances of the Ancient Order of Druids are discussed by North (1931), reviewing Wiese & Fricke 1931, and the subsequent schisms can be followed in numerous ephemeral pamphlets issued by the various groups. Dr Michael Thompson has given me information on the part played at Stonehenge by the Ministry of Public Building and Works (cf. too Atkinson 1960), and Mr Maurice Richardson on Dr Reid.

CHAPTER V

All discussions of prehistoric religion must, of their nature and in the absence of texts, consist of unverified and unverifiable assumptions based on material culture, or by extrapolation beyond the legimate bounds of archaeological inference. The classical texts relating to non-Celtic religions were printed in their original languages by Clemen (1936). For some of the problems of interpretation, cf. Ucko 1962 on the 'Mother Goddess' assumption. Eliade 1964 deals with shamanism in its recently surviving manifestations, and by inference with its possible antecedents. Shamanistic Druids in Ross 1967; hide burials and offerings, Piggott 1962; at La Tène, Jahnkuhn 1966.

Jacquetta Hawkes (1967) summed up the controversy on the use of Stonehenge as an elaborate calendrical computer.

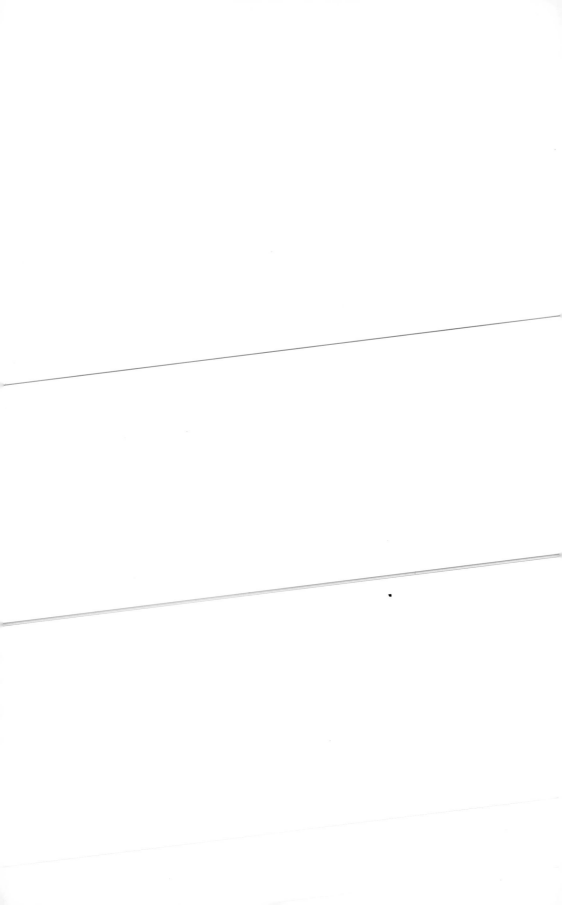

BIBLIOGRAPHY

ALCOCK, L. 1972 *By South Cadbury is that Camelot . . .* (London 1972).

ALFÖLDI, A. 1952 'The Moral Barrier on Rhine and Danube', in Birley, E. (ed.), *The Congress of Roman Frontier Studies 1949* (Durham 1952).

ALLEN, D. F. 1971 · 'British potin coins: a review', in Hill, D., and Jesson, M. (eds), *The Iron Age and its Hill-Forts* (Southampton 1971), 127–159.

D'ARBOIS DE JOUBAINVILLE, H. 1906 *Les Druides* (Paris 1906).

ARNOLD, M. 1867 *On the Study of Celtic Literature* (London 1867).

ASHBEE, P. 1963 'The Wilsford Shaft', *Antiq.* XXXVII (1963), 116–20.

ATKINSON, R. J. C. 1960a *Stonehenge* (Harmondsworth 1960).
1960b *Archaeology, History and Science: an Inaugural Lecture* (Cardiff 1960).

BALDRY, H. C. 1952 'Who Invented the Golden Age?', *Class. Quart.* XLVI (1952), 83–92.

BEATTIE, W. 1967 (National Library of Scotland) *Celtica* (Catalogue of an Exhibition) 1967.

BEHRENS, G. 1930 'Spätlatene Gräber bei Wallertheim', *Germania* XIV (1930), 24–28.

BINCHY, D. A. 1943 'The Linguistic and Historical Value of the Irish Law Tracts', *Proc. Brit. Acad.*

XXIX (1943), 195–227.
1954 'Secular Institutions', in Dillon, M. (ed.), *Early Irish Society* (Dublin 1954), 52–65.
1961 'The Background of Early Irish Literature', *Studia Hibernica* I (1961), 7–18.

BOLTON, J. D. P. 1962 *Aristeas of Proconnesus* (Oxford and New York 1962).

BOWRA, C. M. 1964 'The Meaning of a Heroic Age' (Earl Grey Memorial Lecture 1957), in Kirk, G. S. (ed.), *The Language and Background of Homer* (Cambridge and New York 1964), 22–47.

CHADWICK, N. K. 1966 *The Druids* (Cardiff and Connecticut 1966).

CLEMEN, C. 1936 *Fontes Historiae Religionum Primitivarum* (Bonn 1936).

CUNNINGTON, E. M. & B. H. 1914 'Casterley Camp', *Wilts. Arch. & Nat. Hist. Mag.* XXXVIII (1913–14), 53–105.

DANIEL, D. 1970 Editorial (on Dr William Price of Llantrisant), *Antiq.* XLIV (1970), 86–88.

DANIEL, G. E. 1960 *The Prehistoric Chamber Tombs of France* (London 1960).
1961 Editorial (on Iolo Morganwg), *Antiq.* XXXV (1961), 260–62.

DAVIET, R. 1963 'La Mésure du temps en Gaule', *Rev. Arch. de l'Est & Centre-Est* XIV (1963), 53–80.

DENNING, R. 1963 'Druidism at Pontypridd', *Glamorgan Historian* I (1963), 136–45.

DODDS, E. R. 1951 *The Greeks and the Irrational* (Berkeley 1951).

DOTTIN, G. 1906 *Manuel . . . de l'Antiquité Celtique* (Paris 1906).

DRIEHAUS, J. 1965 'Fürstengräber und Eisenerz zwischen Mittelrhein, Mosel und Saar', *Germania* XLIII (1965), 32–49.

DUDLEY, D. R. & WEBSTER, G. 1962 *The Rebellion of Boudicca* (London and New York 1962).

DUMÉZIL, G. 1935 *Flamen-Brahman* (Paris 1935).
1952 *Les Dieux des Indo-Européens* (Paris 1952).

DUVAL, P. M. 1957 *Les Dieux de la Gaule* (Paris 1957).

ELIADE, M. 1954 *The Myth of the Eternal Return* (London 1954, New York 1965).
1964 *Shamanism: Archaic Techniques of Ectasy* (London and New York 1964).

EVANS, D. E. 1967 *Gaulish Personal Names* (Oxford 1967).

FAIRCHILD, H. N. 1961 *The Noble Savage: A Study in Romantic Naturalism* (New York 1961).

FILIP, J. 1962 *Celtic Civilization and Its Heritage* (Prague and New York 1962).

FORRER, R. 1899. *Heidenmauer von St. Odilien* (Strassburg 1899).

FOWLER, P. J. & EVANS, J. G. 1967 'Plough-Marks, Lynchets and Ancient Fields', *Antiq.* XLI (1967), 289–301.

FOX, A. 1964 *South West England* (London and New York 1964).

FOX, C. 1959 *Life and Death in the Bronze Age* (London and New York 1959).

FRICK, J. G. 1744 *Commentatio de Druidis* (Ulm 1744).

GRANT, M. 1958 *Roman Literature* (Harmondsworth and New York 1958).

GREENE, D. 1954 'Early Irish Society', in Dillon, M. (ed.), *Early Irish Society* (Dublin 1954), 79–92.

GRIFFITHS, J. G. 1956 'Archaeology and Hesiod's Five Ages', *Journ. Hist. Ideas* XVII (1956), 109–19.

GUTHRIE, W. K. C. 1957 *In The Beginning* (London and New York 1957).

HARRISON, W. J. 1901 'A Bibliography of . . . Stonehenge and Avebury', *Wilts. Arch & Nat. Hist. Mag.* XXII (1901), 1–69.

HATT, J. J. 1951 *La Tombe Gallo-Romaine* (Strasbourg 1951).

HAVERFIELD, F. 1900 (Romano-British remains in the Upper Thames Valley), *Proc. Soc. Ant.* 2nd S. XVIII, 1, (1899–1900), 10–16.

HAWKES, C. F. C. 1954 'Archaeological Theory and Method: Some Suggestions from the Old World', *Amer. Anthrop.* LVI (1954), 155–168.
1957 'Prehistory and the Gaulish Peoples', in Wallace-Hadrill, J. M. & McManners, J., *France: Government and Society* (London 1957), 1–18.
1963 'The Celts: Report on the Study of their Culture and their Mediterranean Relations, 1942–62', *Rapp. et Comm. VIIIe. Cong. Internat. d'Arch Class.* (Paris 1963), 3–23.

HAWKES, J. 1967 'God in the Machine', *Antiq.* XLI (1967), 174–80.

HODGEN, M. T. 1964 *Early Anthropology in the Sixteenth and Seventeenth Centuries* (Philadelphia 1964).

HODGES, H. W. M. 1966 'New Views on Papyrus in Pre-Roman Britain', *Antiq.* XL (1966), 308–9.

HOLMES, T. R. 1911 *Caesar's Conquest of Gaul* (Oxford 1911).

JACKSON, K. H. 1953 *Language and History in Early Britain* (Edinburgh and Chicago 1953).
1964 *The Oldest Irish Tradition: A Window on the Iron Age* (Cambridge and New York 1964).

JAHNKUHN, H. 1966 'Zur Deutung der Tierknochenfunde aus La Tène', *Helvetia Antiqua* (Zurich 1966), 155–58.

JANKUHN, H. (ed) 1970 *Vorgeschichtliche Heiligtümer und Opferplätze in Mittel- und Nordeuropa* (Göttingen 1970).

JANSOVÁ, L. 1968 'Mšecke Žehrovice und die Frage der Viereckschanzen in Böhmen', *Arch. Rozh.* XX (1968), 470–488.

JONES, B. 1953 *Follies and Grottoes* (London 1953).

KENDRICK, T. D. 1927 *The Druids: A Study in Keltic Prehistory* (London 1927, New York 1966).
1938 *Anglo-Saxon Art to A.D. 900* (London 1938).
1950 *British Antiquity* (London 1950).

KIMMIG, W. 1965 'Zur Interpretation der Opferszene auf dem Gundestrup-Kessel', *Fundber. aus Schwaben* NF XVII (1965), 135–43.

KIRK, G. S. & RAVEN, J. E. 1957 *The Pre-Socratic Philosophers* (Oxford and New York 1957).

KOEBNER, R. 1941 'The Settlement and Colonisation of Europe', in Clapham, J. H. & Power, E. (eds), *The Cambridge Economic History I* (Cambridge 1941), 1–88.

KÖVES, T. 1955 'Les *Vates* des Celtes', *Acta Ethnog. Acad. Scient. Hung.* IV (1955), 171–275.

DE LAET, S. J. 1966 *Van Grafmonument tot Heiligdom* (Konin. Vlaamse Acad. v. Wettenschappen, Brussels 1966).

LAMBRECHTS, P. 1942 *Contributions à l'Étude des Divinités Celtiques* (Bruges 1942).
1954 *L'Exaltation de la Tête dans la Pensée et dans l'Art des Celtes* (Bruges 1954).

LAST, H. 1949 'Rome and the Druids: A Note', *Journ. Rom. Stud.* XXXIX (1949), 1–5.

LEWIS, M. J. T. 1966 *Temples in Roman Britain* (Cambridge and New York, 1966).

LOVEJOY, A. O. 1936 *The Great Chain of Being* (Harvard 1936).
1948a "The Parallel of Deism and Classicism', in *Essays in the History of Ideas* (Johns Hopkins 1948), 78–98.
1948b 'The First Gothic Revival and the Return to Nature', in *Essays in the History of Ideas* (Johns Hopkins 1948), 136–65.
1948c 'On the Discrimination of Romanticisms', in *Essays in the History of Ideas* (Johns Hopkins 1948), 228–53.

LOVEJOY, A. O. & BOAS, G. 1935 *Primitivism and Related Ideas in Antiquity*, I (Baltimore 1935).

MACNEILL, E. 1928 'On the Notation and Chronography of the Calendar of Coligny', *Eriu* X (1926–28), 1–67.

MANUEL, F. E. 1965 'Towards a Psychological History of Utopias', *Daedalus* (Spring 1965), 293–322.

MARTIN, R. 1965 'Wooden Figures from the Source of the Seine', *Antiq.* XXXIX (1965), 247–52.

MIEROW, C. C. 1966 *The Gothic History of Jordanes* (New York 1962, Cambridge 1966).

MOIR, E. 1964 *The Discovery of Britain: The English Tourists 1540–1840* (London and New York 1964).

MOMIGLIANO, A. 1966a 'An Unsolved Problem of Historical Forgery: the "Scriptores Historiae Augustae"', in *Studies in Historiography* (London 1966), 143–80.
1966b 'Cassiodorus and Italian Culture of his Time', in *Studies in Historiography* (London 1966), 181–210.

MÜLLER-WILLE, M. 1965 *Eisenzeitliche Flüren in den festländischen Nordseegehieten* (Munster 1965).

NEUGEBAUER, O. 1952 'Tamil Astronomy', *Osiris* X (1952), 252–76.
1957 *The Exact Sciences in Antiquity* (Providence 1957).

NILSSON, N. P. 1920 *Primitive Time-Reckoning* (Lund 1920).

NORTH, W. 1931 Review of Wiese & Fricke 1931; *Antiq.* V (1931), 522–23.

OWEN, A. L. 1962 *The Famous Druids* (Oxford and New York 1962).

PALMER, J. 1964 'Rock Temples of the British Druids', *Antiq.* XXXVIII (1964), 285–87.

PEATE, I. C. 1951 'The Gorsedd of the Bards of Britain', *Antiq.* XXV (1951), 13.

PHILLIPS, E. D. 1964 'The Greek Vision of Prehistory', *Antiq.* XXXVIII (1964). 171–78.

PIGGOTT, S. 1950 *William Stukeley: An Eighteenth-Century Antiquary* (Oxford 1950).
1951 'William Camden and the Britannia', *Proc. Brit. Acad.* XXXVII (1951), 199–217.
1955 'The Ancestors of Jonathan Oldbuck', *Antiq.* XXIX (1955), 150–56.
1956 'Antiquarian Thought in the Sixteenth and Seventeenth Centuries', in Fox, L. (ed.), *English Historical Scholarship in the Sixteenth and Seventeenth Centuries* (London 1956), 93–114.
1962 'Heads and Hoofs', *Antiq.* XXXVI (1962), 110–18.
1963 'The Bronze Age Pit at Swanwick, Hants.: a Postscript', *Antiq. Journ.* XLIII (1963), 286–87.
1965 *Ancient Europe: From the beginnings of Agriculture to Classical Antiquity* (Edinburgh and Chicago 1965).
1967 *Celts, Saxons and the Early Antiquaries* (The O'Donnell Lecture 1966: Edinburgh 1967).

PITT-RIVERS, A. 1892 *Excavations in Cranborne Chase III* (London 1892).

POWELL, T. G. E. 1958 *The Celts* (London and New York 1958).

QUINN, D. B. 1966 *The Elizabethans and the Irish* (Cornell 1966).

RICHMOND, I. A. 1950 *Archaeology, and the After-Life in Pagan and Christian Imagery* (Oxford 1950).
1956 'Two Celtic Heads in Stone from Corbridge', in Harden, D. B. (ed.), *Dark-Age Britain* (London 1956), 11–15.

RIETH, A. 1958 'Zur Frage der Bauzeit der Heidenmauer auf dem Odilienberg', *Germania* XXXVI (1958), 113–19.

ROSS, A. 1967 *Pagan Celtic Britain: Studies in Iconography and Tradition* (London & New York 1967).

LE ROUX, F. 1961 *Les Druides* (Paris 1961).

SCHWARZ, K. 1962 'Zum Stand der Ausgrabungen in der spätkeltischen Viereckschanze von Holzhausen', *Jahresber. Bayer. Bodendenkmalpfl.* (1962), 21–77.

SLOTKIN, J. S. 1965 *Readings in Early Anthropology* (London and Chicago 1965).

SMITH, M. A. 1955 'The Limitations of Inference in Archaeology', *Arch. News Letter* VI (1955), 1–5.

STEAD, I. M. 1961 'A Distinctive Form of La Tène Barrow in Eastern Yorkshire and on the Continent', *Antiq. Journ.* XLI (1961), 44–62.

STEINER, P. 1935 'Einbauten in vorgeschichtlichen Gräbern des Trierer Landes', *Trierer Zeitschr.* X (1935), 99–115.

SUMMERSON, J. 1949 'John Wood and the English Town-Planning Tradition', in *Heavenly Mansions* (London 1949, New York 1963), 87–110.

SZABO, M. 1965 'A Celtic Double Head from Badacsony-Labdi', *Acta Arch. Hung.* XVII (1965), 233–50.

TIERNEY, J. J. 1960 'The Celtic Ethnography of Posidonius', *Proc. Royal Irish Acad.* LX (C) (1960), 189–275.

TODD, R. 1946 *Tracks in the Snow: Studies in English Science and Art* (London 1946).

TOYNBEE, J. M. C. 1964 *Art in*

Britain under the Romans (Oxford and New York 1964).

UCKO, P. J. 1962 'The Interpretation of Prehistoric Anthropomorphic Figurines', *Journ. Royal Anthrop. Inst.* XCII (1962), 38–54.

VATIN, C. 1972 'Wooden sculpture from Gallo-Roman Auvergne', *Antiq.* XLVI (1972), 39–42.

VENDRYES, J. 1948 'La religion des Celtes', in *Les Religions de l'Europe* III (Paris 1948).

DE VRIES, J. 1963 *La Religion des Celtes* (Paris 1963).

WHEELER, R. E. M. 1950 'What Matters in Archaeology?', *Antiq.* XXIV (1950), 122–130.

WHITNEY, L. 1934 *Primitivism and the Idea of Progress in English Popular Literature in the Eighteenth Century* (Baltimore 1934 and 1965).

WIESE, H. & FRICKE, H. 1931 *Handbuch des Druiden Ordens* (Munich 1931).

WILD, J. P. 1966 'Papyrus in Pre-Roman Britain?', *Antiq.* XL (1966), 139–41.

WILLEY, B. 1940 *The Eighteenth-Century Background* (London 1940, New York 1941).

DE WITT, N. J. 1938 'The Druids and Romanization', *Trans. & Procs. Amer. Philolog. Ass.* LXIX (1938), 319–32.

ZWICKER, J. 1934 *Fontes Historiae Religioni Celticae* (Berlin 1934).

LIST OF ILLUSTRATIONS

59 Llyn Cerrig Bach gang chain. By permission of the National Museum of Wales, Cardiff.

60 Llyn Cerrig Bach crescentic plaque. By permission of the National Museum of Wales, Cardiff.

61 The Gundestrup cauldron showing drowning. National Museum of Denmark, Copenhagen.

62 Heidelberg head. Badisches Landesmuseum, Karlsruhe.

63 Ex-votos round the spring at Chamalières. Clermont-Ferrand Museum.

64 Wooden votive head from the source of the Seine. Photo R. Rémy.

65 Wooden figure showing internal organs, from Chamalières.

66–67 Wooden votive figures from the source of the Seine. Photos R. Rémy.

68 The Turoe Stone, Co. Galway, decorated with elaborate La Tène style composition. Photo courtesy of E. M. Megaw.

69 Head of wooden phallic figure from Shercock, Co. Cavan. Photo National Museum of Ireland, Dublin.

70 Stone head from Gloucester. City Museum and Art Gallery, Gloucester.

71 Stone head found near Roman road, Appleby, Cumbria. Museum and Art Gallery, Carlisle.

72 Antenociticus head. Museum of Antiquities, University of Newcastle-upon-Tyne.

73 Iron stand with ox-head terminals from Welwyn, Hertfordshire. British Museum. Photo by courtesy of the Trustees.

74 Kul Oba vase, electrotype copy in Victoria and Albert Museum. Photo Peter Clayton.

75 Julius Caesar, coin-portrait on a denarius. British Museum. Photo by courtesy of the Trustees.

76 Engraving of Julius Caesar by W. Dolle.

77 The speech of Caractacus. From *Mona Antiqua Restaurata*, by Henry Rowlands, 1723.

78 The wicker figure. From *Britannia Antiqua Illustrata* by Aylett Sammes, 1676.

79 Simpelveld stone sarcophagus, interior. National Museum of Antiquities, Leiden.

80 Egg capsules of whelk (*Buccinum undetum*), a little larger than life. Photo Douglas P. Wilson.

81 Title-page of Noel Taillepied, *Histoire de l'Estat et Republique des Druides . . .*, 1585.

82 Title-page of Guenebault's *Reveil de l'antique Tombeau de Chyndonax*, 1623.

83 Title-page of Elias Schedius, *De Dis Germanis*, Amsterdam, 1648.

84 Indian in body-paint, by John White. British Museum. Photo by courtesy of the Trustees.

85 War-painted British at the time of Julius Caesar, by Lucas de Heere, 1575. University Library, Ghent.

86 Title-page of Aylett Sammes, *Britannia Antiqua Illustrata*, 1676.

87 Engraving of Druid, from the title-page of Francis Grose, *Antiquities of England and Wales*. 1773–87, vol. IV.

88 Medallion portrait of William Camden. Photo Peter Clayton.

89 Title-page of Inigo Jones, *Stoneheng*, 1655.

90 Stanton Drew stone circle, Somerset. Photo Prof. J. K. St Joseph, Crown Copyright reserved.

91 Illustration of Stonehenge from Walter Charleton, *Chorea Gigantum*, 1663.

92 Title-page of Walter Charleton, *Chorea Gigantum*, 1663.

93 Title-page of Henry Rowlands, *Mona Antiqua Restaurata*, 1723.

94 Plan of moated entrenchment and houses, from Rowlands, *Mona Antiqua Restaurata*.

95 Plan of Circus and associated streets in Bath, designed by John Wood.

96 Plan of Stonehenge by Inigo Jones, 1655.

97, 98 Obverse and reverse of bronze medallion commemorating William Stukeley (1687–1765). Salisbury and South Wiltshire Museum, Salisbury.

99 Projected title-page of William Stukeley, *The History of the Temples of the Ancient Celts*, 1723.

100 Revised version of the same, with 'Druids' instead of 'Celts'.

101 View of Avebury by William Stukeley, drawn in 1723. Photo Peter Clayton.

102 View of Stonehenge by William Stukeley, drawn in 1722. Photo Peter Clayton.

103 'The Druid': opening of autograph of unpublished poem by William Stukeley, 1758.

104 Plaque erected by the East India Company commemorating Prince Lee Boo, Rotherhithe Church, London. Photo A. L. Wood.

105 La Tour-d'Auvergne, Carnac, 1796. British Museum. Photo courtesy of the Trustees.

106 The Heroic Gaul: a late nineteenth-century statue of Ambiorix, Tongres, Belgium.

107 The Unheroic Druid: The Druid Panoramix, from the modern French comic strip series by Goscinny and Uderzo, *Astérix le Gaulois*.

108 The Archdruid of the Welsh Eisteddford, Photo the British Travel Association.

109 The Chief Druid, from Rowlands, *Mona Antiqua Restaurata*, 1723.

110 'Y Derwydd–The Druid'. Air for harp, published by Edward Jones in his *Bardic Museum* of 1802.

111 Title-page of Godfrey Higgins, *The Celtic Druids*, 1827.

112 Title-page of Godfrey Higgins, *The Celtic Druids*, 1829.

113 The Serpent Temple: engraving forming the final page of William Blake's *Jerusalem*, 1804–20.

114 A Mythological Trilithon: from William Blake's *Jerusalem*, 1804–20.

115 Mont de la Ville, Jersey, now rebuilt at Park Place, Henley-on-Thames. From Britton and Brayley, *Beauties of England and Wales*, 1802.

116 An Archdruid in his Judicial Habit. Coloured aquatint from S. R. Meyrick and C. H. Smith, *The Costume of the Original Inhabitants of the British Islands*, 1815.

117 Druid, Rocking Stone and Mistletoe at Rishworth, Yorkshire, 1773.

118 The Megalithic Folly at Ilton, Yorkshire. Drawing by Barbara Jones.

119 Cover illustration on sheet music of a quadrille arranged by Charles d'Albert, showing Norma and her father the Archdruid.

120 Production of Bellini's *Norma* at La Scala Theatre, Milan, 1964–5. Photo Eric Piccagliani, Milan.

121 Costume of the Druidical order. Coloured aquatint from S. R. Meyrick and C. H. Smith, *The Costume of the Original Inhabitants of the British Islands*, 1815.

122 Portrait of Dr William Price of Llantrisant. This formed the frontispiece of his *Gwylellis yn Nayd* (The Will of My Father), 1871. By permission of the National Museum of Wales, Welsh Folk Museum, Cardiff.

123 Cremation of Dr William Price at Caerlan, Llantrisant, 1893. By permission of the National Museum of Wales, Welsh Folk Museum, Cardiff.

124 Dr William Price in costume. The translation of the two poems is in *Ap Idanfryn Dr Price of Llantrisaw* by Nicholas (not dated).

125 Modern Druids celebrating the Summer Solstice at Stonehenge, June 1968. Photo Picturepoint.

126 The induction of Winston Churchill into the Albion Lodge of the Ancient Order of the Druids at Blenheim, 1908. Photo *The Oxford Times*.

127 Druids on Tower Hill in London, 1964. Photo *The Observer*.

128 Plan of the wagon-grave at Vix, after Joffroy and Piggott.

129 Painting by Holman Hunt (1827–1910), *A Christian Missionary Sheltering from the Druids*. Department of Western Art, Ashmolean Museum, Oxford.

130 Wine label illustrating a Druid: Vin des Druides, Château du Chayne.

Line drawings prepared by Dr Morna Simpson.